ACCA
NEW SYLLABUS
PRACTICE & REVISION KIT

Paper 1.3

Managing People

BPP Publishing
August 2001

First edition August 2001

ISBN 0 7517 0787 2

British Library Cataloguing-in-Publication Data
A catalogue record for this book
is available from the British Library

Published by

BPP Publishing Limited
Aldine House, Aldine Place
London W12 8AW

www.bpp.com

Printed in Great Britain by Ashford Colour Press

We are grateful to the Association of Chartered Certified Accountants for permission to reproduce past examination questions. The answers to past examination questions have been prepared by Claire Wright on behalf of BPP Publishing Limited.

CONTENTS

BPP PUBLISHING

Question and answer checklist/index

The headings in this checklist/index indicate the main topics of questions, but questions often cover several different topics.

All questions are exam-standard questions.

Questions preceded by * are **key questions** which we think you must attempt in order to pass the exam. Tick them off on this list as you complete them.

You will see that all scenario questions are key questions. This is because they are compulsory and can be quite wide-ranging in coverage,

BPP PUBLISHING

TOPIC INDEX

Listed below are the key Paper 1.3 syllabus topics and the numbers of the questions in this Kit covering those topics.

If you need to concentrate your practice and revision on certain topics or if you want to attempt all available questions that refer to a particular subject (be they preparation, exam-standard or case study/scenario-based questions), you will find this index useful.

The New Syllabus *Managing People* paper differs from the Old Syllabus *Organisational Framework* in a number of ways. Some of the questions in this kit are on topics which were not covered under the Old Syllabus, and these are marked with an asterisk (*).

The old *Organisational Framework* syllabus focused principally on the organisation and the environment. This paper focuses much more on the role of the manager. If for whatever reason, you have studied (or sat) *Organisational Framework* but are sitting *Managing People* in December 2001, you will need to cover the new areas or those which are covered in more depth.

- Management and supervision
- Teams
- Recruitment and relation
- Training and development

In fact, the bulk of the syllabus is new; only the coverage on organisations, motivation and leadership is generally equivalent to the former *Organisational Framework* paper.

RETAKE STUDENTS SHOULD PAY PARTICULAR ATTENTION TO THE QUESTIONS ON THE TOPIC AREAS MARKED WITH A *. THESE ARE BEING EXAMINED FOR THE FIRST TIME UNDER THE NEW SYLLABUS.

	Syllabus topic	Question numbers
*	**A**ppraisal	32, 33, 34
	Authority	14
*	**B**ehaviour	12
	Bureaucracy	3
	Bureaucratic structures	4
	Centralisation	2
*	Communication	44, 45, 46, Mock Exam 2 (Pilot Paper)
*	Conflict	48, Mock Exam 1
*	Counselling	47
	Culture	8, 9
	Decentralisation	2
	Delegation	16, Mock Exam 1
*	Disciplinary action	49
*	Discrimination	26
*	Diversity	27
*	**E**mployee development	29
	Empowerment	5, Mock Exam 1
*	Equal opportunities	28
*	**G**rievance interview	50
*	Groups	11

(vi)

Syllabus topic	Question numbers
★ **H**ealth and safety	35, 36
★ **I**nduction	30
★ Informal organisation	10
★ Interpersonal relationships	13
★ Interviews	24
★ **J**ob advertisement	22
★ Job analysis	Mock Exam 2 (Pilot Paper)
★ Job descriptions	21, Mock Exam 1, Mock Exam 2 (Pilot Paper)
★ Job design	39
Leaders	41, 42, 43, Mock Exam 1
Leadership	14, Mock Exam 1
Leadership style	42
★ Learning organisation	Mock Exam 1
★ Learning process	31
★ Learning styles	31, Mock Exam 2 (Pilot Paper)
Management	6, 14
★ Managerial roles	5
Managers	41
★ Maslow	38
Matrix organisation	1
Mintzberg	5
★ Motivation	38, 39, 40
Motivator factors	39
New organisation	4
★ **O**bjectives	17
Organisation structure	1
★ **P**ay and rewards	39, 40, Mock Exam 2 (Pilot Paper)
★ Perception	13
★ Performance management	19, Mock Exam 1
★ Person specification	Mock Exam 1, Mock Exam 2 (Pilot Paper)
Power	14
★ **R**ecruitment	20, 25, Mock Exam 2
★ Responsibility	15
★ Rewards	39, 40, Mock Exam 2
★ Roles	13
★ **S**election	23, 25
★ Social responsibility	18
★ Stress	37
★ Supervisor	7
Teams	11, 43, Mock Exam 2 (Pilot Paper)
Theory X	38
Theory Y	38
★ Training	29, Mock Exam 2

THE EXAM PAPER

Approach to examining the syllabus

The examination is a **three hour paper** constructed in **two sections.**

Section A consists of a brief scenario with a number of questions totalling 40 marks. Each question carries two marks and all questions must be attempted. Section A is compulsory.

Section B consists of five essay type questions, with one question taken from each of the five topics in the syllabus. Each question carries 15 marks and all candidates must attempt four questions.

There are no calculations involved, and candidates should note that the answers in Section B **must be presented in essay form** (BPP emphasis). Candidates need to show an understanding of the detail of the topic. Candidates should be aware that although the course is made up of a number of discrete topics, examination questions may well require a knowledge of more than one of these topics.

		Number of Marks
Section A	Compulsory scenario question	40
Section B	Choice of 4 out of 5 essay questions (15 marks each)	60
		100

Additional information

The Study Guide provides more detailed guidance on the syllabus.

Analysis of pilot paper

Section A

1   Case study based on recruitment of a new member of staff to an accounts department

Section B

2   Teams and informal groups
3   Job analysis
4   Learning styles
5   Rewards and motivation
6   Communication

HOW TO PASS PAPER 1.3

Revising with this Kit

A confidence boost

To boost your morale and to give yourself a bit of confidence, **start** your practice and revision with a topic that you find **straightforward**.

Key questions

Then try as many as possible of the **exam-standard questions**. Obviously the more questions you do, the more likely you are to pass the exam. But at the very least you should attempt the **key questions** that are highlighted in the questions and answer checklist/index at the front of the Kit. Even if you are short of time, you must prepare answers to these questions if you want to pass the exam - they incorporate the key techniques and concepts underpinning *Managing People* and they cover the principal areas of the syllabus.

Keep to time

The scenario question is worth 40 marks. So if you find you have spent significantly less than 70 minutes, you must have missed something. This paper is not difficult, but you do have to keep to time. The other questions are worth 15 marks or 27 minutes.

Presentation, presentation, presentation

You will make it easier to mark if you present the answer well, with clear paragraphs, subheadings and so on. It is easier to mark. But remember, you normally have to explain matters so most of the time a bullet point approach is not enough.

No cheating

Produce **full answers** under **timed conditions**; practising exam technique is just as important as recalling knowledge. Don't cheat by looking at the answer. Look back at your notes or at your BPP Study Text instead. Produce answer plans if you are running short of time.

Imagine you're the marker

It's a good idea to actually **mark your answers**. Don't be tempted to give yourself marks for what you meant to put down, or what you would have put down if you had time. And don't get despondent if you didn't do very well. Refer to the **topic index** and try another question that covers the same subject.

Ignore them at your peril

Always read the **Tutor's hints** in the answers. They are there to help you.

Trial run for the big day

Then, when you think you can successfully answer questions on the whole syllabus, attempt the **two mock exams** at the end of the Kit. You will get the most benefit by sitting them under strict exam conditions, so that you gain experience of the four vital exam processes.

- Selecting questions
- Deciding on the order in which to attempt them
- Managing your time
- Producing answers

Recent articles

The content of any relevant articles published before February 2001 is reflected in the BPP Study Text for *Managing People*. Articles published since then which are of direct relevance to the syllabus are listed below. We have also included articles devoted to the Certified Accounting Technician C6 *Managing People,* as it has a lot in common with the Professional scheme syllabus for 1.3.

'Use your appraisal to get ahead', Judi Geisler, *Student Accountant,* February 2001, pages 4-5.

'Let's get motivated', Seam Purcell, *Student Accountant,* February 2001, pages 7-8.

'Disciplinary and grievance procedures', S R Das Gupta, *Student Accountant,* February 2001, pages 26-28.

USEFUL WEBSITES

The websites below provide additional sources of information of relevance to your studies for *Financial Reporting*.

- ACCA   www.accaglobal.com
- BPP   www.bpp.com
- Financial Times   www.ft.com

BPP PUBLISHING

SYLLABUS MINDMAP

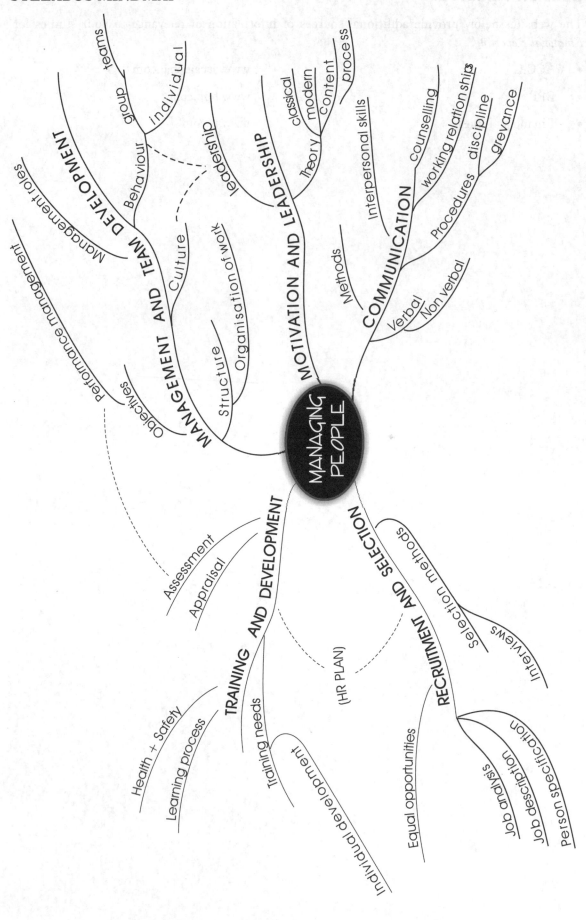

OXFORD BROOKES

The standard required of candidates completing Part 2 is that required in the final year of a UK degree. Students completing Parts 1 and 2 will have satisfied the examination requirement for an honours degree in Applied Accounting, awarded by Oxford Brookes University.

To achieve the degree, you must also submit two pieces of work based on a **Research and Analysis Project.**

- A 5,000 word **Report** on your chosen topic, which demonstrates that you have acquired the necessary research, analytical and IT skills.

- A 1,500 word **Key Skills Statement,** indicating how you have developed your interpersonal and communication skills.

BPP was selected by the ACCA to produce the official text *Success in your Research and Analysis Project* to support students in this task. The book pays particular attention to key skills not covered in the professional examinations.

> AN ORDER FORM FOR THE NEW SYLLABUS MATERIAL, INCLUDING THE OXFORD BROOKES PROJECT TEXT, CAN BE FOUND AT THE END OF THIS STUDY TEXT.

MBA

Plans for a new joint MBA have been announced by the ACCA and Oxford Brookes University. This new qualification will be available worldwide from 2001.

It follows the existing agreement between ACCA and Oxford Brookes to offer ACCA students the opportunity to qualify for BSc in Applied Accounting. Both institutions have now agreed to strengthen links through the development of a postgraduate qualification designed for ACCA members. Preliminary work has begun on the new MBA.

For further information, please see the ACCA's website: www.acca.org.uk

Questions

MANAGEMENT AND TEAM DEVELOPMENT

Questions 1 to 19 cover Management and Team Development, the subject of Part A of the BPP Study Text for Paper 1.3.

---

1   ORGANISATION STRUCTURE
27 mins

All organisations have some kind of formal structure.

Required

(a) What are the purposes of a formal organisation structure?   **5 marks**
(b) What factors influence the structure of an organisation?   **5 marks**
(c) Briefly describe the principles of 'matrix' organisation.   **5 marks**

Total marks = 15

2   CENTRALISATION AND DECENTRALISATION
27 mins

Centralisation and decentralisation refer to how authority is distributed in an organisation.

Required

(a) Describe the main advantages and disadvantages of centralisation.   **10 marks**
(b) What factors influence the extent of decentralisation in an organisation?   **5 marks**

Total marks = 15

3   BUREAUCRACY
27 mins

It has been claimed that the organisational models of the past are no longer appropriate for the fast-changing corporate context of today and tomorrow.

Required

(a) Outline the main criticisms of bureaucracy as an organisational form.   **10 marks**
(b) Suggest why bureaucracy continues to survive in many organisations.   **5 marks**

Total marks = 15

4   NEW ORGANISATION
27 mins

It has been suggested that the rigidity of bureaucratic structures makes them dysfunctional in a fast-changing, competitive environment.

Required

Describe five ways in which work can be organised more flexibly, so that organisations can be more responsive to customer demands and environmental changes.   **15 marks**

5   SCENARIO: MANAGERIAL ROLES
72 mins

XYZ Ltd is a medium-sized firm manufacturing components for industrial markets. Under its new Managing Director, John Nakimura, it has recently undergone a major change programme.

Work had previously been organised according to scientific management principles, but XYZ has now introduced teamworking and empowerment. The workforce has welcomed

3

the programme of multi-skill training and team-building exercises, and is beginning to take responsibility for meeting output and quality targets set by management.

The managers, however, appear to be highly stressed by the changes. They report feeling that the business is 'slipping out of their control'. You have been recently appointed as Assistant Human Resource Manager to XYZ Ltd and have been asked by Mr Nakimura to plan a training and counselling programme for managers.

Required

(a) Outline the shortcomings of the scientific management approach, with reference to any subsequent theory you think relevant. **10 marks**

(b) List the roles of the modern manager, according to Henry Mintzberg and describe underlying assumptions about managerial work. **10 marks**

(c) Suggest how Mintzberg's theory may be helpful to XYZ's managers. **5 marks**

(d) Explain the benefits of empowerment. **8 marks**

(e) Outline how the managers' role is changed by empowerment. **7 marks**

Total Marks = 40

6   MANAGEMENT THEORY *27 mins*

The process of management has been described in terms of its basic functions.

Required

(a) Describe the functions of management, according to a named management theorist of your choice. **10 marks**

(b) Discuss any omission or special emphasis you find interesting in the theory you have cited. **5 marks**

Total Marks = 15

7   THE SUPERVISORY ROLE *27 mins*

The number of employees in the accounting office has grown to such an extent that an office supervisor is required. The chief accountant understands management – but is unclear as to the role of a supervisor.

Required

(a) Explain the difference between the roles of a supervisor and a manager. **5 marks**
(b) Describe the main duties and responsibilities of a supervisor. **10 marks**

Total Marks = 15

8   MANIFESTATIONS OF CULTURE *27 mins*

Organisation culture has been defined as the complex body of shared beliefs, attitudes and values in an organisation.

Required

(a) Describe how culture manifests itself, giving examples. **8 marks**
(b) Suggest why culture is important to an organisation. **7 marks**

Total Marks = 15

9   TYPES OF CULTURE   *27 mins*

It has been suggested that organisations can be classified, according to their structures, processes and management methods, into four distinct cultural types.

Required

(a) Describe the distinctive features of:

    (i)   Task culture   **3 marks**
    (ii)   Role culture   **3 marks**
    (iii) Power culture   **3 marks**
    (iv) Person culture   **3 marks**

(b) Identify the factors which influence which culture an organisation will develop.

                                                     3 marks

                                  Total Marks = 15

10   INFORMAL ORGANISATION   *27 mins*

Alongside every formal organisation structure, there is an informal structure.

Required

(a) What is meant by the term 'informal organisation'?   **4 marks**

(b) What are the benefits of the 'informal organisation' for overall organisational effectiveness?   **5 marks**

(c) What are the dangers of the 'informal organisation' and how can they be minimised?   **6 marks**

                                  Total Marks = 15

11   SCENARIO: GROUPS AND TEAMS   *72 mins*

LMN Ltd is a small marketing services agency. Work is allocated to multi-disciplinary project or account teams comprising 8 to 10 people: specialists in marketing research, copywriting, design, project co-ordination and so on.

You have been put in charge of a new project team, formed from other teams which have recently disbanded. It is the second week the team has been together, and progress on the task is frustratingly slow. There are lots of creative ideas being put forward, but team members criticise everything and try to put their own ideas over others'.

Your manager is getting concerned and asks you to report on how the team is working.

Required

(a) Explain the stages of team formation, identifying which stage your team has reached.

                                      10 marks

(b) List the various roles that you will be trying to develop in your team, in order for it to function effectively.   **10 marks**

(c) Propose three measures for encouraging cohesion in your team.   **9 marks**

(d) Outline the drawbacks to creating a very cohesive team.   **6 marks**

(e) State what you understand 'successful' teamworking to mean.   **5 marks**

                                  Total Marks = 40

12   INDIVIDUAL BEHAVIOUR

27 mins

Individual behaviour is different from group behaviour.

Required

(a) Explain the impact on work behaviour of:

     (i)   Personality factors   **5 marks**
     (ii)   Attitudes   **5 marks**

(b) In what ways might individual work contribution be more effective than group or team working?   **5 marks**

Total Marks = 15

13   ROLES AND PERCEPTIONS

27 mins

You have just attended a seminar entitled 'Reading the signs', on the topic of perception and role theory, and have been asked by your manager to share what you have learned.

Required

(a) Explain what you understand by the terms:

     (i)   Perception   (2 marks)
     (ii)   Roles   (2 marks)

(b) Write brief guidelines for staff on how to avoid interpersonal clashes due to differences of perception.   (6 marks)

(c) Explain how roles influence interpersonal relationships at work.   (5 marks)

(15 marks)

14   AUTHORITY AND POWER

27 mins

'Management is about authority; leadership is about power.'

Required

(a) What do the terms 'authority' and 'power' mean in this statement?   **4 marks**
(b) From where do managers derive their authority?   **4 marks**
(c) From where do leaders derive their power?   **7 marks**

Total Marks = 15

15   AUTHORITY AND RESPONSIBILITY

27 mins

'Authority without responsibility creates tyrants. Responsibility without authority creates martyrs.'

Required

Explain what you would expect to be the results of a mismatch between delegated authority and responsibility in an organisation.   **15 marks**

16 ENCOURAGING DELEGATION

27 mins

As a result of company expansion, your accounts manager seems to be working a lot of overtime hours and taking work home. At the same time, you and three other accounts assistants are underutilised.

Required

(a) Explain why delegation is necessary.   **3 marks**
(b) Explain why managers may be reluctant to delegate.   **7 marks**
(c) How can this reluctance be overcome?   **5 marks**

Total Marks = 15

17 THE PURPOSE OF OBJECTIVE SETTING

27 mins

'Objectives are needed in every area where performance and results directly and vitally affect the survival and prosperity of the business.' (Peter Drucker)

Required

(a) Explain what you understand by the term 'objectives'.   **3 marks**
(b) What are the organisational purposes of setting objectives?   **4 marks**
(c) What are the behavioural purposes of setting objectives?   **5 marks**
(d) Give three examples of organisational objectives.   **3 marks**

Total Marks = 15

18 SOCIAL RESPONSIBILITY

27 mins

'The only justification for social responsibility is enlightened self-interest.' (Milton Friedman)

Required

(a) Explain the benefits to a business of socially responsible policies.   **8 marks**

(b) List areas in which an organisation might formulate socially responsible and ethical objectives.   **7 marks**

Total Marks = 15

19 PERFORMANCE MANAGEMENT

27 mins

'Performance management is a means of getting better results... by understanding and managing performance within an agreed framework of planned goals, standards and competence requirements.' (Armstrong)

Required

(a) Outline the process of performance management.   **8 marks**
(b) How can goals, standards and competence requirements be determined?   **7 marks**

Total Marks = 15

RECRUITMENT AND SELECTION

Questions 20 to 28 cover Recruitment and Selection, the subject of Part B of the BPP Study Text for Paper 1.3.

20   RECRUITMENT RESPONSIBILITIES

27 mins

Your organisation wishes to recruit a number of new accounts staff.

Required

(a) Describe the role of the Human Resources department in recruitment.   **5 marks**

(b) Describe the role of Recruitment consultants.   **5 marks**

(c) What factors would the organisation take into account in deciding whether to use consultants.   **5 marks**

Total Marks = 15

21   JOB DESCRIPTION

27 mins

Your organisation has just redesigned several jobs and you have been asked whether you think it is necessary to draw up job descriptions for them.

Required

(a) What are the uses and benefits of job descriptions?   **8marks**
(b) What are the limitations and drawbacks of job descriptions?   **7 marks**

Total Marks = 15

22   JOB ADVERTISEMENT

27 mins

Your organisation wishes to advertise a vacancy for an accounts assistant, and you have been asked to advise on the best way to go about this.

Required

(a) Draft guidelines on what makes an effective job advertisement.   **9 marks**
(b) Evaluate some options for advertising media relevant to this vacancy.   **6 marks**

Total Marks = 15

23   SCENARIO: SELECTION METHODS

72 mins

FGH Ltd has advertised a vacancy for a Payroll Assistant in the Accounts Department, and has received a number of cvs and letters.

The new Human Resource Manager, Sandra Cunningham, has been reviewing the personnel records of the firm and has noted that FGH uses interviews as its sole selection method. The records further show that a number of new recruits have left the firm within two years of employment, and that training and development costs for recruits in their first three years appear to be disproportionately high.

Ms Cunningham is concerned that the firm's selection methods are failing to match candidates to the realistic requirements of vacancies. She asks you, as her assistant, to prepare some notes for her to present to the management team.

Required

(a) Outline the qualities of an effective job application form.   **7 marks**

(b) Explain the limitations of interviews as a selection method.   **10 marks**

(c) Recommend a range of other techniques that could be used in selection.   **10 marks**

(d) What kind of information should the organisation seek in checking the references of candidates?   **5 marks**

(e) Suggest four other measures that could be used to improve the success of FGH's selection procedures.   **8 marks**

Total Marks = 40

24   INTERVIEWS

27 mins

Most firms use the interview as their main tool for selection decisions.

Required

(a) What are the purposes of selection interviewing?   **5 marks**

(b) Describe the factors to be taken into account in using a selection interview effectively.   **10 marks**

Total Marks = 15

25   EVALUATING RECRUITMENT AND SELECTION

27 mins

Your organisation is planning an audit of its HR practices. You have been asked to recommend ways of evaluating recruitment and selection procedures.

Required

(a) Outline four methods of evaluating recruitment and selection.   **8 marks**

(b) List seven performance indicators of effective recruitment and selection procedures.   **7 marks**

Total Marks = 15

26 AREAS OF DISCRIMINATION

27 mins

The range of discrimination issues has widened in recent years.

Required

(a) Describe the grounds on which discrimination is unlawful or subject to regulation (with reference to a country of your choice) **10 marks**

(b) Distinguish between direct and indirect discrimination under UK law **5 marks**

Total Marks = 15

27 MANAGING DIVERSITY

27 mins

Your organisation has decided to develop its policy on diversity in employment. The Accounts Manager has had advice on 'equal opportunity', but is not sure that she understands all the issues involved in 'diversity'.

Required

(a) Explain how a 'managing diversity' approach might be different from an equal opportunities policy. **10 marks**

(b) Suggest five ways of creating and supporting diversity at work. **5 marks**

Total Marks

28 EFFECTIVE EQUAL OPPORTUNITIES POLICY

27 mins

Your organisation advertises itself as an 'equal opportunities employer' in recruitment literature, but it appears to you that it does only the bare minimum to comply with the law.

Required

(a) Outline a five-step plan to make the claim a reality. **10 marks**

(b) List five specific measures to encourage job and/or training applications by different groups who are otherwise disadvantaged in employment. **5 marks**

Total Marks = 15

> **TRAINING AND DEVELOPMENT**
>
> Questions 29 to 37 cover Training and Development, the subject of Part C of the BPP Study Text for Paper 1.3.

29   SCENARIO: TRAINING   *72 mins*

JIK Ltd is a retail chain selling camera equipment and supplies to professionals and the general public. Feedback surveys completed by its customers have recently highlighted customer service problems, including 'ignorant or uninformed staff' and 'indifferent or inattentive staff'.

JIK has traditionally recruited photography enthusiasts to work in its stores and has not so far felt the need to offer training in either technical knowledge or customer service skills. The Manager of one store, Matthew Hlavcek, has been heard to say: 'Photographers know what they want, and they know that can get it from us. Training is a waste of time and resources.'

As the newly-appointed assistant manager of at Hlavcek's store, you decide that the feedback surveys give sufficient impetus for you to recommend a new attitude to training.

Required

Draft a report for Matthew Hlavcek, outlining the following.

(a)   What you consider to be the benefits of training to:

    (i)   The organisation   **5 marks**
    (ii)   The individual   **5 marks**

(b)   How you would identify the training needs of staff.   **10 marks**

(c)   What methods you would choose to satisfy the training needs of staff.   **8 marks**

(d)   How you would carry out evaluation of training methods.   **6 marks**

(e)   What you understand by the term 'employee development'.   **6 marks**

Total Marks = 40

30   INDUCTION   *27 mins*

Attitude surveys used among staff in your organisation have highlighted the perception that it is difficult to 'fit in' in the first year of employment. You have been asked to consider introducing formal induction programmes for new recruits.

Required

(a)   What are the advantages and disadvantages of formal induction?   **8 marks**
(b)   Suggest a format for a formal induction course.   **7 marks**

Total Marks = 15

31   THE LEARNING PROCESS   *27 mins*

Organisations often seem to believe that just 'doing training' is a good thing, but there are different learning styles and approaches which suit different individuals.

Required

(a) Identify and describe two different schools of though on approaches to learning.

4 marks

(b) What does learning theory suggest about the requirements of effective training programmes?   **5 marks**

(c) Identify and describe Honey and Mumford's learning styles.   **6 marks**

Total Marks = 15

32   PURPOSES AND OBJECTIVES OF APPRAISAL   *27 mins*

You are leading a management seminar in an organisation which is considering the introduction of a formal performance appraisal system. The following points are raised during question time: show how you would respond to each one.

(a) 'The only point of having appraisal is setting pay awards, and we already have job evaluation to do that.'   **8 marks**

(b) 'Our managers give informal feedback to their staff every day: why have a formal system?'   **7 marks**

Total Marks = 15

33   TRENDS IN APPRAISAL   *27 mins*

Appraisal schemes have been criticised as being backward-looking, perfunctory, perpetuating 'top-down' control and irrelevant to performance in the job.

Required

Identify and describe three new approaches to appraisal which may address the issues raised in these criticisms.   **15 marks**

34   EVALUATING APPRAISAL   *27 mins*

A survey of employers by Saville and Holdsworth indicated the mixed success of appraisal schemes in meeting objectives. How might an organisation go about appraising the effectiveness of its own appraisal procedures?

Required

Suggest what factors or outcomes should be monitored, and identify the criteria to be evaluated by each.   **15 marks**

35 THE IMPORTANCE OF HEALTH AND SAFETY   *27 mins*

Much of the EU and UK legislation and regulation in regard to employment concerns the issues of health and safety at work.

Required

(a) Explain why health and safety at work are important.   **8 marks**

(b) Why might there be health and safety problems in the workplace, despite law and regulation?   **7 marks**

Total Marks = 15

36 THE COST OF ACCIDENTS   *27 mins*

Newspapers frequently quote statistics showing large numbers of employee hours lost through accidents, and the associated cost to business.

Required

(a) List the potential costs to employers of accidents at work   **8 marks**

(b) Outline steps which can be taken to reduce the frequency and severity of accidents.

7 marks

Total Marks = 15

37 STRESS   *27 mins*

New issues in occupational health and safety are constantly arising as the organisational environment changes: stress has been identified as a major health issue in recent years.

(a) Briefly describe the symptoms of stress.   **5 marks**

(b) Briefly describe the causes or aggravators of stress.   **5 marks**

(c) List some of the techniques available for managing stress.   **5 marks**

Total Marks = 15

BPP
PUBLISHING

> **MOTIVATION AND LEADERSHIP**
>
> Questions 38 to 43 cover Motivation and Leadership, the subject of Part D of the BPP Study Text for Paper 1.3.

38   SCENARIO: THEORIES OF MOTIVATION   *72 mins*

PQR Ltd is a firm providing computer maintenance services. It employs a number of engineers on flexible contract agreements: a basic number of guaranteed hours per week, supplemented by freelance work. It also employs full-time office staff.

Ben is one of the engineers: in his late twenties, married with two young children, and studying computer programming part-time. Anne is a book-keeper: 50 years old, widowed and living alone, she had several years' book-keeping experience with a larger company before leaving work to raise children.

You are mentor to one of the staff managers, Brigitte Bosch. She has recently attended a seminar on motivational theory and has come to ask your help. 'I wanted to know how to motivate people like Anne and Ben, and I've been asked to re-evaluate our reward system,' she says, 'but what with 'content' and 'process' and 'X' and 'Y', I was just confused. The only theory I found easy to grasp was the hierarchy of needs: perhaps I can use that?'

Required

(a) Distinguish between content and process theories of motivation.   **6 marks**
(b) Explain Theory X and Theory Y.   **6 marks**
(c) Critically evaluate Maslow's hierarchy of needs theory.   **6 marks**
(d) Identify the likely motivational issues for Anne and Ben.   **10 marks**
(e) Outline the management objectives of an effective reward system   **12 marks**

    Total Marks = 40

39   THE JOB AS A MOTIVATOR   *27 mins*

'Dissatisfaction arises from environment factors: satisfaction can only arise from the job.' (Herzberg)

Required

(a) Distinguish between environmental and motivator factors.   **3 marks**

(b) Evaluate three methods of job design for their ability to offer intrinsic rewards.

    12 marks

    Total Marks = 15

40   PAY AS A MOTIVATOR   *27 mins*

Frederick Herzberg identified pay as a hygiene factor in his motivational model.

Required

(a) Evaluate the effectiveness of pay as a motivator.   **7 marks**

(b) Describe four methods or criteria by which an organisation may determine the level and structure of the monetary rewards it offers its employees.   **8 marks**

    Total Marks = 15

41   MANAGERS AND LEADERS   *27 mins*

'Managers are necessary; leaders are essential.' (Viscount Slim)

Required

(a)   Describe what is meant by the term 'leadership'   **4 marks**
(b)   Distinguish between 'management' and 'leadership' activities   **6 marks**
(c)   Explain why 'leadership' is important in business organisations.   **5 marks**

Total Marks = 15

42   LEADERSHIP STYLE   *27 mins*

'Choosing a leadership style which is entirely appropriate to any given situation is one of the most important skills that an effective manager can possess.'

Required

Critically discuss this statement, giving reasons for your views.   **15 marks**

43   TEAMS AND LEADERS   *27 mins*

Contingency approaches to leadership take into account not just leadership traits and styles but wider aspects of the leadership situation.

Required

(a)   Outline the 'Action-centred leadership' model.   **10 marks**

(b)   Explain the role of the leader in Handy's contingency theory of team effectiveness.
5 marks

Total Marks = 15

> **EFFECTIVE COMMUNICATION PRACTICES**
>
> Questions 44 to 50 cover Effective Communication Practices, the subject of Part E of the BPP Study Text for Paper 1.3.

44   SCENARIO: IMPROVING COMMUNICATION IN ORGANISATIONS

72 mins

TUV Ltd is a firm which undertakes road reconstruction and maintenance. The work is carried out by teams which operate independently of each other and on-site, spending little time at head office.

As a team co-ordinator, you have investigated a number of recent customer complaints about delays and misunderstandings. It appears that instructions given to head office are not reaching the teams quickly or clearly enough, although both sales staff and work planners deny the problem. The teams respond that they have raised concerns about co-ordination time after time at bi-monthly 'planning committee' meetings, but nothing ever gets done: the committee is 'all talk, no action' – and the teams come away feeling that head office lacks understanding of their work and respect for their input.

You identify the problem as poor communication on many levels. The Managing Director, John Macgraith, asks you to draft a training programme to improve communications at TUV.

Required

(a) Explain the importance of good communication   **8 marks**

(b) List ten major barriers to good communication.   **10 marks**

(c) Suggest how these barriers can be overcome.   **7 marks**

(d) Explain the particular problems of upward communication in an organisation and suggest how upward communication can be improved.   **10 marks**

(e) Give brief guidelines on how TUV can improve its planning committee.   **5 marks**

Total Marks = 40

45   COMMUNICATION MEDIA AND METHODS   *27 mins*

The choice of communication methods and media which are appropriate the purpose of communication and the needs of the target audience is an important skill in effective communication.

Required

(a) List the five main communication methods, giving examples of appropriate media for each method.   **8 marks**

(b) What factors influence the choice of communication media in a given situation?

7 marks

Total Marks = 15

46   ORAL AND NON-VERBAL SKILLS   *27 mins*

Research findings suggest that managers spend more time listening and reading or speaking.

Required

(a) Draft guidelines for managers on how to be effective listeners.   **8 marks**

(b) Draft guidelines for managers on how to improve their effectiveness as 'non-verbal communicators'.   **7 marks**

Total Marks = 15

47   COUNSELLING   *27 mins*

'Counselling can be defined as a purposeful relationship in which one person helps another to help himself.' (Rees)

Required

(a) Explain the purposes of counselling in an organisation.   **5 marks**
(b) Draft some 'dos' and 'don'ts' to guide managers in counselling staff.   **10 marks**

Total Marks = 15

48   IDEOLOGIES OF CONFLICT   *27 mins*

From different perspectives, conflict can be seen as destructive or constructive; as a fact of organisational life or as a problem to be avoided.

Required

(a) Outline three basic viewpoints on conflict.   **9 marks**
(b) List the potential constructive and destructive effects of conflict.   **6 marks**

Total Marks = 15

49   DISCIPLINARY ACTION   *27 mins*

The accounts manager wants to be liked by his work team, but also wants to be respected. He knows that discipline is necessary, but is uncomfortable with the idea of punishment. He asks for your advice.

Required

(a) What do you understand by the term 'discipline' at work?   **5 marks**

(b) In what circumstances might disciplinary action be required?   **5 marks**

(c) Identify five principles for managing the interpersonal aspects of disciplinary action.
                                                                          5 marks

Total Marks = 15

50   GRIEVANCE INTERVIEW

27 mins

A grievance occurs when an individual thinks that he or she has been wrongly treated by colleagues or supervisors. The purpose of formal grievance procedures is to resolve the problem to the satisfaction of all concerned.

Required

(a)   Outline the process of a grievance interview.   **10 marks**

(b)   List the matters that should be stated in a formal grievance policy.   **5 marks**

Total Marks = 15

Answers

1   ORGANISATION STRUCTURE

> **Tutor's hint.** This is a straightforward question if you read the topic and instruction key words carefully. In part (a) they are the *purposes* of *formal* organisation *structure*. In part (b) they are the *factors* which *influence* the structure. In part (c) they are the *principles* of *matrix* organisation. Get used to rationing yourself to 5 marks' worth of relevant points per part, so that you have time to complete all parts of the question.

(a)   **Purposes of formal organisation structure**

The formal structure of an organisation is designed to provide a framework for the controlled performance of collective goals. This framework is intended to perform the following functions.

    (i)   **Link individuals and teams** in a consistent network of relationships so that the flow of authority, responsibility and communications can be controlled and predicted.

    (ii)   **Provide a structure for the allocation of tasks** and accountabilities to individuals and teams within functionally specialised or other forms of organisation.

    (iii)   **Allocate to each individual or team the authority** required to perform the tasks and accountabilities allocated to them, by virtue of positional or legal power.

    (iv)   **Co-ordinate and control the objectives, activities and use of resources** of individuals and teams within the organisation, so that overall aims are achieved without gaps or overlaps in accountability or flow of work.

    (v)   **Facilitate the flow of work**, information and other resources through the organisation by establishing communication channels.

(b)   **Factors influencing organisational structure**

There are a number of ways of looking at this question.

    (i)   Fayol, for example, suggested that organisations should be structured according to certain **universal, rational principles**: division of work (or specialisation), a scalar chain of authority and responsibility, unity of command and unity of direction.

    (ii)   Mintzberg, on the other hand, suggested that organisations have **different ways** of relating to their work and **different methods of co-ordination** and that organisational preferences in these areas shape the structure.

    (iii)   A contingency theory of structure suggests that a number of variables influence organisation structure, including:

        •   Its age

        •   Its size and geographical dispersion

        •   The nature of the task and technology

        •   The type of personnel employed

        •   Organisational values and strategies (eg a belief in teamworking or empowerment)

        •   Environment (eg requiring a flexible, or supporting an inflexible, structure).

(c)   **Principles of matrix organisation**

Matrix organisation 'crosses' functional and product/customer/project organisational forms into a system of dual authority. Members of functional departments remain under the direct line authority of their department heads: at the same time, they are under the authority of a product or project manager for their work on the relevant product or project (whether on an on-going basis, or as part of a temporary team).

Matrix organisation thus facilitates inter-disciplinary co-operation, co-ordination and communication, allowing greater flexibility and responsiveness to changing requirements.

A geographically-based matrix may be illustrated as follows.

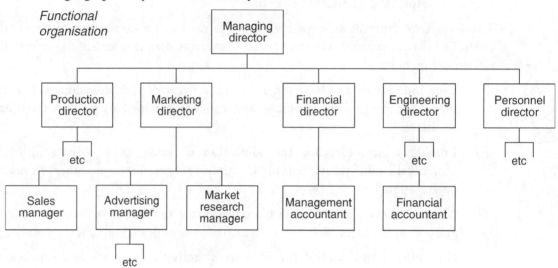

2   CENTRALISATION AND DECENTRALISATION

> **Tutor's hint.** The introduction to the question indicates the sense in which the terms centralisation and decentralisation are being used. Make sure you know which is which (centralisation = less delegation, decentralisation = more delegation) and note that part (a) refers only to one term and part (b) to the other.

(a) **Advantages and disadvantages of centralisation**

A centralised organisation is one in which authority is concentrated at what Mintzberg called the strategic apex: lower levels of the hierarchy have little decision-making authority and merely carry out instructions or set procedures.

Advantages

(i)   **Decisions are made at one point**, and so may be made more quickly (particularly important in crisis) and with better control and consistency.

(ii)   **Senior managers** in an organisation can take **a wider view** of the objectives, problems and consequences of decisions for the whole organisation: they see 'the big picture'.

(iii) Senior management can **balance the needs and interests of different units** and stakeholders of the organisation, where there might otherwise be political competition and conflict.

(iv)   The quality of decisions should (theoretically) be higher due to senior managers' skills, experience and access to wider sources of information.

(v)   There may be a **reduction in the cost of management overheads.**

Disadvantages

(i)   Senior managers may be **overloaded** in terms of workload and the stress of responsibility.

(ii)   Lower **levels of management may be demotivated** by the absence of opportunities to exercise authority or develop their roles.

(iii)   The organisation may **fail to develop managerial successors** and skills in entrepreneurship, initiative and innovation which are crucial in a fast-changing market environment.

(iv)   **Head office managers may lack local and front-line knowledge** to respond to customer requirements and the realities of working conditions.

(v)   **Slow decision making.** Decisions required by changing operational and customer demands are slowed down by the need to refer them upwards.

(b)   **Factors influencing the extent of decentralisation**

Geographical dispersion and remoteness from the centre encourages a degree of autonomy, although information technology can reduce the effects of physical distance for co-ordination.

An organisation with a **variety of activities**, markets and/or product ranges may benefit from decentralisation, as varying specialist skills and knowledge will be required to manage different processes.

Competition and rapid environmental change will necessitate **decentralisation**, in order to speed up the organisation's response to customer demands and technological and market developments.

The **management style** and organisational culture will either support delegation/decentralisation or discourage it (in a 'power' culture, for example).

The **capabilities of the organisation's managers** will support or hinder decentralisation, according to whether they are able to deal with devolved responsibility, able to delegate effectively and so on.

3   BUREAUCRACY

> **Tutor's hint.**   The introduction sets the context for this question: the need for organisations to move from rational efficiency (and rigidity) to more flexible forms which allow them to respond to environmental changes and customer demands. Part (a) should be familiar territory: part (b) perhaps less so. It invites you to think about some of the benefits offered by bureaucracy and about some of the ways in which bureaucracy perpetuates itself, by its very nature.

(a)   **Criticisms of bureaucracy**

(i)   The **complexity of decision-making** (eg to obtain the go-ahead for new projects or responses to customer demands) slows down the process, causing delays and rigidity and conflicting with increasing customer demands for flexibility and quick responses.

(ii)   **Rigidity.** Behavioural **conformity creates ritualism and formalism**, inhibiting the development of individuals. Individuals may become frustrated and demotivated.

(iii)   **Inflexibility.** Rules and procedures, once internalised, tend not to adapt to changing goals and environmental pressures and can become irrelevant or dysfunctional 'red tape' (Merton).

(iv)   **No learning.** The control mechanism (whereby feedback on errors are used to initiate corrective action) is hampered by the rigidity and complexity of communication channels, so that the organisation is unable to learn from its mistakes (Crozier).

23

(v) Bureaucracies take an **inward-looking orientation**, focused on procedures and rituals ('inputs') rather than customer needs, performance and results ('outputs'): they are therefore incapable of responding without trauma to fast-changing environments.

(vi) Because of these various forms of rigidity, bureaucracies are **bad at innovation**: they repress creativity and initiative.

(vii) Bureaucracies tend to be **tall organisations** and tend to require a lot of 'red tape': this can result in over-staffing, inefficiency and diseconomies of scale, at a time when competitive organisations are delayering and downsizing. A classic example is the National Health Service: despite chronic shortages of nurses and doctors, 300,000 more administrators are required to run the NHS today than twenty years ago.

(b) **Reasons for the survival of bureaucracy**

Not all bureaucracies are bad.

(i) Bureaucracy is acknowledged to **foster efficiency and consistency** of performance, high technical competence and strong esprit de corps (Weber).

(ii) Bureaucracy work well in environments characterised by **slow-changing** technologies, lack of competition, plentiful labour (or scarce employment) and authoritarian values.

(iii) The **impersonality, rationality and procedures** of bureaucracy suit the desire of employees for **fairness and security**, and the demand for organisations to comply with **laws and regulations** (eg on health and safety or employment protection).

(iv) Bureaucracy is **self-perpetuating**, because it recruits and retains managers and employees who like the structured, predictable environment.

(v) Bureaucracy is self-perpetuating, because it fails to learn from its mistakes and is slow to change.

4   NEW ORGANISATION

> **Tutor's hint.** There are a number of ways you could approach this question. You could discuss flexible working ('core' and 'peripheral' staffing, for example, and flexible working hours). You could outline specific flexible structures: matrixes, multi-disciplinary and multi-skilled teams and so on. We have opted for a broad survey of the new flexible organisational forms.

Flexible organisation structures

Flexibility has become a key issue in organisation and human resource management, as increasing competition has empowered customers and organisations have been forced to respond more flexibly to customer demands and expectations, technological changes and competitive pressures. Recent trends in flexible organisation include the following broad strands.

(a) **Flattening hierarchies**

Flat structures are **more responsive**, because there is a more direct relationship between the organisation's strategic centre and the operational units at the interface with the customer.

Flattening involves **delayering**: cutting out levels of organisation which lengthened the lines of communication and decision-making, encouraged specialisation (as opposed to functional versatility) and limited the authority of customer-facing staff to mobilise resources to competitive advantage.

(b) **Horizontal structures**

Horizontal structures allow work to be shared between different functions of a business by breaking down barriers. Specialisation, especially where enshrined in formalised job descriptions and departments, created barriers to the flow of information and resources within the organisation. By **softening these barriers, attention would be focused on getting the job done,** satisfying the customer, solving the problem and so on – rather than on the processes of communication and organisational politics. Horizontal structures include multi-functional project teams, multi-skilling and matrix structures.

(c) **Chunked structures**

'Chunking' means creating **smaller** (and therefore more flexible) **units within the organisation structure**, through team-working and empowerment.

Handy's 'shamrock' organisation which divides the workforce into a permanent **core**, an **inner periphery** of flexible part-time or temporary labour and an **outer periphery** of sub-contractors: this allows labour to be deployed more flexibly and efficiently according to fluctuating work requirements. The extreme form of this approach is what Peters calls 'unglued' structures: loose networks of autonomous, entrepreneurial project teams which constantly form and reform according to requirements.

(d) **Output-focused structures**

The key to all the above trends is the **focus on outputs** (notably, customer satisfaction and loyalty) **rather than internal processes** and functions (as in bureaucratic forms). Project management structures, for example, exist to further the target outcomes of the project and are then renewed or changed at the end of the project.

(e) **Jobless structures**

People's contributions are increasingly flexible and goal-directed rather than defined (and potentially constrained) by job descriptions and demarcations. At the same time, long-term continuity of employment (allowing career planning) is less prevalent. Some go as far to say that the job is a thing of the past: employees need to have a portfolio of competencies which can be used flexibility for one employer or, on a freelance basis, for a succession of employers. Some organisations develop their people for 'employability' rather than for narrow competence in a particular task, job or career.

5 SCENARIO: MANAGERIAL ROLES

> **Tutor's hint.** The scenario suggests that XYZ's managers have rather rigid expectations about the managerial role and task, based on their previous experience of scientific management, in which their separateness from and control over the workers would have been emphasised. Empowered teamworking represents a radical change of role and culture. The managers need to learn that management is not a neat matter of systematic planning, instructing and controlling: hence the relevance of Mintzberg's theories (particularly to part (c)). They also need to understand the shift from compliance to commitment as the guiding principle of organisational control: hence the critique of scientific management (which we have made from the human relations point of view, since Mayo and others were direct critics of their predecessors) and the justification of empowerment. If there is no longer a place for commanding, instructing and controlling, managers must adopt more facilitating roles. This kind of general analysis of the scenario will help to focus your answers for each of the question parts. Don't forget to address specific theories, when asked to do so.

(a) **Shortcomings of the scientific management approach**

Context

Scientific management was based on the micro-design of jobs and the assumption that workers would accept and learn to perform simple, repetitive tasks 'properly' **in return** for **increases in pay**.

Scientific management fell out of favour when human relations theorists (such as Maslow and Herzberg) became interested in the motivational aspects of the job itself and the role of 'job satisfaction' in employee performance.

(i) It was recognised that, contrary to Taylor's assumptions, **monetary reward was not the only incentive to work** performance: Herzberg demonstrated that pay was only a 'hygiene' factor, prone more to creating dissatisfaction than lasting satisfaction.

(ii) It was also recognised that jobs made up of low-skilled, repetitive **are socially isolating, meaningless** and monotonous for the worker: Elton Mayo's Hawthorne experiments suggested that social relationships and responsibility raised both morale and performance levels.

These factors pose problems for management.

(i) **Monotony and boredom** contribute to 'industrial fatigue'. Tasks which provide little mental stimulation may cause accidents and errors.

(ii) High workload, low discretion jobs - such as the micro-designed jobs resulting from Taylorism – have been associated with **worker stress** and associated absenteeism.

(iii) **Motivation and morale suffer** from lack of challenge, variety and meaning in the work itself, despite efforts to offer monetary compensation for the lack of job satisfaction.

(iv) Where meaningless tasks are perceived to be the lot of the worker, under the control of management, **employee relations** may be subject to resentment and conflict.

(v) By assuming that workers have no knowledge to contribute to their work, and by depriving them of an understanding of the wider context of their work, the **organisation misses out on a key source of energy, creativity, customer awareness** and first-hand experience of work systems and processes.

(vi) Given advances in motivational theory and practice since Taylor, worker expectations of the 'quality of working life' have been raised: organisations managed according to Taylor's principles may have trouble attracting and retaining skilled staff.

(b) **Mintzberg's managerial roles**

Mintzberg suggested that in their daily working lives, managers fulfil three types of managerial role.

(i) *Interpersonal roles*

- Figurehead: representing the organisation to the outside world
- Leader: managing human resources
- Liaison: making contacts within the organisation, across functional boundaries

(ii) *Informational roles*

- Monitor: gathering information from the environment
- Spokesperson: providing information on behalf of the team or organisation
- Disseminator: passing information on to subordinates and colleagues

(iii) *Decisional roles*

- Entrepreneur: evaluating opportunities and initiating projects
- Disturbance handler: responding to problems and conflicts
- Resource allocator: deciding where to direct scarce resources
- Negotiator: obtaining resources and decisions in the interests of the team

Mintzberg's studies and conclusions debunked several myths about managerial work.

(i) Managers are not reflective, systematic planners.

(ii) Managerial work is disjointed and discontinuous.

(iii) Managers have routine duties to perform: not all 'routine tasks' are the job of junior staff.

(iv) Management is not, in fact, a 'science': it is the practice of judgement and intuition, gained from experience in particular situations: it cannot be analysed and codified.

(c) **Mintzberg's theory and XYZ's management**

Implications

(i) This may reassure XYZ's management that their fear of matters 'slipping out of their control' merely reflects the real world nature of management.

(ii) It may help them to realise that their expectations of an environment in which the managerial job is separate, systematic and controllable are unrealistic.

(iii) It may show them that their work is not, after all, of a different and superior kind to that of the production workers, but interwoven with it.

(iv) It may show them that the principles according to which they have so far managed are not universally recognised, and that in many ways the managerial task is more various, more personal and more meaningful than they have previously thought.

All these ideas may help to motivate XYZ's managers to consider new roles in the light of the change programme.

(d) **Benefits of empowerment**

(i) Empowerment makes much more effective use of the human resource. If employees are treated as if they have something to contribute and can be trusted to exercise responsibility once they are committed to organisational goals (Theory Y), the organisation can:

- Harness effort and creativity among the people who actually do the work

- Take advantage of the front-line exposure and knowledge of customer-facing and production workers to solve the problems and identify opportunities

- Reap cost and efficiency savings from delayering and flexible working methods

BPP PUBLISHING

- Benefit from a climate of commitment rather than compliance, including more co-operative employee relations, flexibility and willingness to embrace change

Empowerment puts decision-making closer to the customer and to the product. It thus cuts down on unnecessary communication, speeds decision-making and enhances the organisation's responsiveness to customer needs and environmental changes. It enables horizontal organisation – crossing functional and job barriers in order to get the job done – which reflects customer experience and helps foster customer satisfaction and loyalty.

Empowerment also increases employee satisfaction and loyalty, and may help attract and retain high-calibre labour to the organisation, which is especially important in areas of skill shortage.

Empowerment does not imply 'free rein': it can be made to function meaningfully (for the above benefits) within decision-making parameters acceptable to management.

(e) **The managers' role in empowerment**

Instead of securing the compliance of operational staff with top-down authority, and instructing them in the 'right' way of doing their jobs, managers will have a more facilitative role.

Managerial role in empowered organisations

(i) Monitoring and disseminating the information required by the team to do its job

(ii) Sourcing material, equipment, finance, skills and other resources for the team

(iii) Networking and negotiating on behalf of teams within the organisation, in the competition for finite resources

(iv) Supporting team members in problem-solving, for example by mobilising training resources or offering counselling and coaching

(v) Inspiring and motivating team members to their best performance, through goal articulation, the creation of guiding values (culture), persuasion and other interpersonal processes of leadership

(v) Co-ordinating the values, activities and resources of the organisation as a whole to support shared objectives

Empowerment does not mean managers no longer manage. Instead, they manage in a different way. Managers have been freed up by empowerment for a more interpersonal, cultural and strategic focus. They are beginning to learn new skills (in change management, leadership and so on) that have a far longer shelf-life than the exercise of traditional managerial functions.

6   MANAGEMENT THEORY

Tutor's hint. Don't forget to name the theorist of your choice! We have selected Drucker – as probably the less popular option: his distinctive contributions (part (b)) are to argue that the *basic* function of the manager of a business is economic performance, and to emphasise the importance of communication in all management functions. You may have chosen to discuss Henri Fayol, and his five functions: planning, organising, commanding, co-ordinating and controlling. In part (b), you may then have commented on the absence of communicating in Fayol's framework, and/or on how 'commanding' has largely been overtaken by ideas about 'motivating' or 'leading' in the modern environment of management.

(a) **Functions of management**

Peter Drucker worked in the 1940s and 1950s as a professional business adviser and was a prolific writer on organisations and management.

He categorised the **functions of management** broadly as follows.

- Managing the business
- Managing managers
- Managing workers and work

Drucker grouped the **work of managers** into five categories.

(i) **Setting objectives for the organisation**. Managers decide what the mission and aims of the organisation and its units should be, quantify targets for achievement, and communicate those targets to other people

(ii) **Organising the work**. The tasks of the organisation must be grouped and divided into manageable activities, expressed as projects or jobs. These must be integrated in turn into a formal organisation structure and allocated to appropriate individuals and teams.

(iii) **Motivating employees** and communicating information to them to enable them to do their work.

(iv) **Measuring work**. Managers co-ordinate the control cycle in the organisation: establishing objectives or yardsticks of performance; analysing actual performance and appraising it against the objectives and targets; communicating the findings, and explaining their significance, so that adjustments can be made.

(v) **Developing people**. The manager 'brings out what is in them or he stifles them. He strengthens their integrity or he corrupts them'.

Drucker argued that every manager performs all five functions, whether well or badly.

(b) **Distinctive contributions of Drucker's classification of management functions**

Drucker noted that the basic function of the manager of a business is **economic performance**: this sets the business manager apart from the manager of other types of organisation. Management can only justify its existence and authority by the economic results it produces – whatever significant non-economic benefits are also gained (such as employee morale or ethical business practices).

Drucker also emphasised the **importance of communication** in the functions of management. This distinguishes his classifications from those of Henri Fayol. Fayol's 'commanding' function, for example, is quite different in character to Drucker's 'motivating' and 'developing people': Drucker's roles are much **closer to the modern definition of leadership,** with its emphasis on the interpersonal roles of the manager in gaining commitment, not just compliance with organisational directives. Likewise, Drucker's approach to the 'measuring' of work is a more facilitative process than Fayol's 'control', although it also describes a control system.

7 THE SUPERVISORY ROLE

> **Tutor's hint.** The supervisor has a unique role as an *interface* between management and workers. This is the essential factor in any discussion of the supervisory role.

(a) **Difference between supervision and management**

As the supervisor's job is a junior management job, the tasks of supervision are similar to those of management, but supervision has **several distinguishing features.**

(i) Supervisors are **usually front line managers,** dealing directly with the levels of the organisation where the basic work is done. They therefore deal with matters such as health and safety at the operational level, while managers may deal with such matters primarily at a strategic or policy-making level.

(i) Supervisors are the **interface between workers and management**: their subordinates are non-managerial employees, whereas managers may manage lower levels of management.

(iii) Supervisors do not spend all their time on the managerial aspects of the job, as they have their **own technical or operational work to perform.**

(iv) Supervisors monitor and control work by means of day-to-day, frequent and detailed information. Higher levels of management plan and control using longer-term and less detailed information (reporting by exception).

(b) **Main duties and responsibilities of a supervisor**

(i) **Planning.** The supervisor is responsible for operational work planning for the department, so as to meet work targets set by more senior management. This will involve scheduling of operations for people and equipment, resource allocation and, where appropriate, the training and induction of staff.

(ii) **Organising and overseeing** the work of others. This may involve: the requisitioning of materials; ordering new equipment; authorising expenditure; monitoring work flow and re-ordering work priorities; allocating jobs; providing coaching and mentoring; and maintaining liaison with more senior management.

(iii) **Controlling,** or making sure the work is done properly. This may involve: keeping job records and time sheets; monitoring quality standards; attending progress control meetings; dealing with disciplinary and performance problems of staff; ensuring the work procedures and health and safety rules are observed; checking the progress of new recruits and trainees; ensuring that work targets are achieved; reporting any deviations from plans and to management targets.

(iv) **Motivating** team members to maintain or improve work performance. This may involve the supervisor in front-line human resource management: articulating goals and standards; recommending or administering reward bonus schemes; identifying training and development opportunities; involving staff (where appropriate) in decision-making affecting their work; counselling and supporting staff members in the event of difficulties; reporting to management on the concerns of staff; consulting with staff representatives in areas of concern.

(v) **Communicating upwards** (on behalf of team members to management), downwards (on behalf of management to team members) and laterally (with other sections): briefings and instructions; consultations; advocacy for staff issues; work flow information from other departments and so on.

(vi) **'Doing'**: supervisors have their own operational and problem solving work.

8   MANIFESTATIONS OF CULTURE

> **Tutor's hint.** Note that this question does not give you any excuse for discussing different types or classifications of organisational culture. It asks you for the ways in which culture manifests or shows itself: some hints are already given in the introduction to the question. It then asks you to suggest why culture is important: it is, in fact, inevitable (every organisation has a culture) but what *effects* – positive or negative – might it have that would lead an organisation to want to *manage* its culture to its benefit.

(a) **Manifestations of culture**

Definition

Handy sums up 'culture' as 'that's the way we do things round here'. For Schein, it is 'a pattern of basic assumptions that... have worked well enough to be considered valid and, therefore, to be taught to new members as the correct way to perceive, think and feel'.

Ways in which culture is manifested

(i)   **Beliefs, values and attitudes.** For example, values about quality or the customer ('the customer is king'), attitudes towards rules, change, risk ('Slow and steady wins the race') and so on. Attitudes and values will be reflected in the kind of people the organisation employs (their age, education and personality), the degree of delegation and communication and so on.

(ii) **Customs:** acceptable ways of behaving, sometimes enforce by written or unwritten rules. The formality of relationships, dress and ways of speaking are a classic example. Communication and decision-making styles (collaborative or command-and-control) are more complex customs.

(iii) **Artefacts:** visible products and tools through which the organisation expresses its 'style'. The style of the offices or other premises, the corporate identity expressed in letterheads and logos, dress codes, display 'trophies' and so on are visible signs of how the organisation regards itself.

(iv) **Rituals:** formal, repeated behaviours that take on special significance. Organisations may use 'ceremonial' behaviours to open meetings, to congratulate successful performers, to celebrate staff birthdays and so on.

(v)   **Symbols:** signs which express values and attitudes. Symbols include the 'badges of status' which are prized in the organisation: a corner office, access to executive facilities, company cars and so on. They may, however, be tied into the mythology of the organisation.

(b) **The importance of culture**

(i)   It affects the motivation and satisfaction of employees. A positive culture can encourage commitment to the organisation and its objectives, make employees feel valued and trusted and use 'guiding values' instead of rules.

(ii) It affects the adaptability of the organisation. A positive culture can encourage innovation, acceptable risk-taking, sensitivity to the environment, customer care, willingness to try new methods and technologies and so on.

(iii) It affects the organisation's image in the outside world, and particularly its appeal to potential employees and customers.

(iv) It affects specific areas of operation. 'Macho' cultures, for example, have been shown to encourage unacceptable levels of risk-taking in regard to health and safety.

31

(v) It creates a predisposition which may undermine attempts at behavioural change. Peters, for example, suggested that IBM's attempts to decentralise were undermined by an essentially bureaucratic culture.

9 TYPES OF CULTURE

> **Tutor's hint.** This question helpfully steers you in the right direction by naming the cultural models (Harrison/Handy) that you need to discuss: just make sure you attach the right description to the right label! You may have had to think a little harder about part (b), but some of the factors in the four types may have jogged your memory.

(a) **Task culture** (identified with the goddess Athena by Charles Handy) is focused on **outputs**. It is reflected in **project teams and task forces**, in which the principal concern is to get the job done: functional barriers and leadership roles are subordinated to the desire to mobilise information and resources for results. Expertise is a prized value in task cultures, and **performance is judged according to results**. Task cultures can be expensive to maintain, as there is a high market value on expertise, innovation, flexibility and learning.

Role culture (identified with the god Apollo) is a bureaucratic culture, founded on rational principles of organisation. **It is focused on processes.** Apollonian cultures have a formal, specialised, hierarchical structure and operate according to well-established rules and procedures. This makes them extremely consistent and stable in their performance and behaviour. Individuals are required to perform their roles with technical competence, within the strict bounds of their positional authority: the role culture offers a **high degree of security and esprit de corps, but tends to squash initiative and innovation.**

Power culture (identified with the god Zeus) is focused on the **boss**. Power and influence stem from a central source, often the owner-directors or founders of the business. There are **few rules**, procedures and formal structures, because **the central control is so strong and dynamic**: this makes power cultures capable of adapting quickly to meet change. They are best suited to **smaller entrepreneurial organisations**, where the leaders have a direct communication with all employees: the leader's influence decreases as the size of the organisation increases. In order to function effectively in such a culture, personnel have to get on well: power cultures are also **called 'club cultures' because they tend to be collections of 'like-minded people...** working on empathetic initiative with personal contact'.

Person culture (identified with the god Dionysus) centres on the interests of the individuals within the organisation, rather than on task goals or organisational processes. Person culture is comparatively rare, but can be seen in chambers of barristers (in the UK), creative partnerships, artists co-operatives and so on: the **management of the business is often seen as an ancillary function designed to support the key individuals.**

These four cultures do not equate to specific organisation types: it is quite possible for different cultures to prevail in different parts of the same organisation with different tasks and orientations.

(b) **Factors influencing culture**

(i) **The organisation's history**. Culture reflects the values of the times in which the organisation was founded, the values and assumptions of its founders, and also the gathering of stories, rituals and customs over time, which act as a powerful source of the organisation's self-perception.

(ii)   **Leadership style.** Leaders are 'creators and sellers of culture' (Pettigrew). Culture is perpetuated by the organisation's tendency to recruit and develop managers who 'fit'.

(iii) **Size.** As organisations grow larger, they tend to rely less on personal communication and more on standardisation for control: hence the tendency toward role cultures.

(iv)   **Task and technology.** Different tasks and technologies demand different levels of flexibility and different structural/cultural forms (Burns and Stalker, Woodward and others).

(v)   **Environment.** A wide range of competitive, technological and social factors will contribute to organisational culture. Customer and employee expectations, for example, have led to a shift towards task cultures.

10   INFORMAL ORGANISATION

> **Tutor's hint.** The introduction to the question raises the important point that formal and informal organisations co-exist: managers do not have a choice of whether to have or allow an informal organisation. Understanding and managing the informal organisation (as far as possible) will therefore be valuable. If you correctly identified what was meant by the term 'informal organisation', the rest should be straight forward, but note that part (c) is really two questions in one.

(a)   **Informal organisation**

Unlike the formal organisation, the **informal organisation** is loosely structured, flexible and spontaneous. It embraces such mechanisms as:

(i)   Social relationships and groupings (eg cliques) within – or across – formal structures

(ii)   The 'grapevine', 'bush telegraph', or informal communication which by-passes the formal reporting channels and routes

(iii) Behavioural norms and ways of doing things, both social and work-related, which may circumvent formal procedures and systems (for good or ill). New members must 'learn the ropes' and get used to 'the way we do things here'

(iv)   Power/influence structures, irrespective of organisational authority: informal leaders are those who are trusted and looked to for advice

(b)   **Benefits of the informal organisation**

(i)   The meeting of employees' social needs may contribute to **morale and job satisfaction,** with benefits in reduced absenteeism and labour turnover.

(ii)   **Knowledge sharing.** The availability of information through informal networks can give **employees a wider perspective** on their role in the task and the organisation, potentially stimulating 'big picture' problem-solving, cross-boundary co-operation and innovation.

(iii) **Speed.** Informal networks and methods may **sometimes be more efficient in achieving** organisational goals, where the formal organisation has rigid procedures or lengthy communication channels, enabling decisions to be taken and implemented more rapidly.

(iv)   The directness, information-richness and flexibility of the informal organisation may be particularly helpful in conditions of rapid **environmental change,** facilitating both the mechanisms and culture of anti-bureaucratic responsiveness.

(v)   The formation and strengthening of interpersonal networks **can facilitate teamworking and co-ordination across organisational boundaries.** It may reduce organisational politics – or utilise it positively by mobilising effective decision-making coalitions and by-passing communication blocks.

(c)   **Managing the informal organisation**

Each of the positive attributes of informal organisation could as easily be detrimental if the power of the informal organisation is directed towards goals unrelated to, or at odds with, those of the formal organisation.

(i)   **Social groupings may act collectively against organisational interests**, strengthened by collective power and information networks. Even if they are aligned with organisational goals, group/network maintenance may take a lot of time and energy away from tasks.

(ii)   The **grapevine is notoriously inaccurate** and can carry morale-damaging rumours.

(iii)   The **informal organisation can become too important** in fulfilling employees' needs: individuals can suffer acutely when excluded from cliques and networks.

(iv)   Informal work practices may **'cut corners'**, violating safety or quality assurance measures.

Such dangers can be minimised by:

(i)   Meeting employees' needs as far as possible via the formal organisation: providing information, encouragement, social interaction and so on

(ii)   Harnessing the dynamics of the informal organisation – for example by using informal leaders

(iii)   Involving managers in the informal structure so that they support information sharing, the breaking down of unhelpful rules and so on

11   SCENARIO: GROUPS AND TEAMS

> **Tutor's hint.** The theoretical content of the questions should be familiar to you, once you have identified the topic key words. In part (a), 'stages of team formation' should be a clear pointer to the work of Tuckman. In part (b), 'various roles' should suggest the work of Belbin. In parts (c) and (d), 'cohesion' should focus your attention on team building and the dangers of groupthink. Part (e) asks you to define team success: don't forget to consider this from the point of view of the team members as well as the organisation. In terms of the scenario, note that your team is newly formed: you should recognise the portrait of a team in the 'storming' stage of formation. Any team-building measures you propose should take into account the new, temporary and multi-functional nature of your team: don't treat it as if it were a permanent, homogenous department.

(a)   **Team formation**

All teams go through various stages before they become fully formed as a functioning team. Four stages were identified by Tuckman.

Forming is the first stage, when the group is just coming together and may still be seen as a collection of individuals while its purpose, composition and organisation are being established. Individuals will be trying to find out about each other, and about the aims and norms of the group. There will at this stage probably be a wariness about introducing new ideas, sticking out or rocking the boat.

Storming is the next stage, which frequently involves more or less open conflict between group members, as changes are agreed in the original objectives, procedures and norms, and as candidates for leadership of the group compete for influence. People begin to risk putting forward ideas, options and solutions.

Norming is a period of settling down. There will be agreements about work sharing, individual roles and output expectations. Group procedures and customs will be defined and adherence to them secured by the group's power to bring members into line. A reasonable hearing is given to everyone and consensus sought on decisions.

Performing is the stage at which the group sets to work to execute its tasks. Even at earlier stages, some performance will have been achieved, but the fourth stage marks the point at which the difficulties of growth and development no longer absorb the group's energies and the group is able to focus on results.

The project team appears to be at the storming stage of development, since there are plenty of ideas being put forward, but in a rather competitive spirit, resulting in conflict: members are still testing out their roles and influence within the group. I am not worried about the conflict and slow progress at this early stage for these reasons.

- It is a normal and necessary process of team formation.

- It is a constructive process, allowing team members to get to know each other, to establish workable roles and to set realistic working relationships and targets, so that the group can move to the norming and performing stages.

(b) **Roles to be developed within the team**

The team is deliberately multi-functional, embracing skills and experience in different creative, technical and administrative disciplines: team members have been selected to occupy specific, complementary **functional** roles required by the project. However, in terms of effective team-working, there is also a range of **process** roles that need to be fulfilled.

Belbin suggested that there are eight necessary roles, which should ideally be balanced and evenly distributed within the team. I will therefore attempt to identify, steer and develop team members in the following roles as the 'norming' stage of team formation progresses. (Some members may exercise more than one role, or move from one role to another as required by the situation: this is merely a framework.)

(i) **Co-ordinator** (or chairman): presides over and co-ordinates team activity, being balanced, disciplined and good at working through others.

(ii) **Shaper:** spurs the team on to action, being dominant, extraverted and passionate about the task.

(iii) **Plant:** provides the team with imaginative ideas and proposals, being introverted but creatively intelligent.

(iv) **Monitor-evaluator:** dissects ideas and spots potential problems and flaws in the team's thinking, being more analytically intelligent.

(v) **Resource-investigator:** accesses new contacts, information and resources for the team, being a sociable, extraverted networker, though not an originator.

(vi) **Implementer** (or company worker): translates ideas into working methods, scheduling, planning and so on: a practical organiser – not a leader, but an essential administrator.

(vii) **Team worker**: holds the team together, by being quietly supportive and understanding of members' needs and smoothing potential conflict with diplomacy.

(viii) **Completer-finisher**: keeps an eye on the details, 'chivvies' the team to meet its deadlines and makes sure that tasks are followed up where necessary.

In addition, we may need to co-opt various experts to fulfil the role of Specialist, if we run into particular problems: we are already a team of relevant specialists in the disciplines required by the project.

(c) **Three measures for encouraging cohesion**

As outlined above, cohesion should naturally increase once the team has progressed through its 'storming' phase. However, the following team-building measures may facilitate this process.

(i) **Reinforce the group's sense of identity**

Since we are a temporary project group, it will not be possible to build a collective history or long-term badges of identity. However, I propose that we adopt the meetings room allocated for our briefings as a Team Headquarters, so we can have our own space, marked by our charts, resources and so on. Introducing all members to the client will also reinforce team identity.

(ii) **Reinforce team solidarity (loyalty, trust, relationships)**

Again, we will not have a long history together, so it is essential to accelerate relationship-building by expressing solidarity; encouraging informal communication between team members (perhaps by out-of-work social contact); dealing with conflict swiftly and openly; and controlling competition by treating everyone fairly. If possible, we could also establish an element of competition with other project groups: perhaps offering a prize for the best client evaluation.

(iii) **Reinforcing commitment to shared team objectives**

The project depends on team member co-operation, so this should be easy to emphasise. I propose to set out team objectives clearly, and to allow the team to participate in setting tactics and targets; to seek and give regular feedback on progress and on the client's responses; to celebrate (and, with the partners' approval) reward all group achievements.

(d) **Drawbacks to ultra-cohesive teams**

The dangers of teams becoming too attached to group maintenance activities, at the expense of task activities, are well researched. The phrase 'group think' was coined by Janis to describe a situation in which a group becomes completely absorbed with its own maintenance, members and priorities, and is blinkered to what is going on around it. The implications of this for task performance is as follows.

(i) The desire for consensus within the group, and hostility to outsiders, may **prevent consideration of alternatives**, constructive criticism or dissenting views. This can lead to **complacent and risky decision-making**.

(ii) The **sharing of responsibility** for decisions further leads to **riskier decision-making.**

(iii) Ultra-cohesive groups **focus a lot of their energies on member satisfaction**, potentially at the expense of task objectives.

(iv) Attachment to existing group processes and membership may **create hostility towards newcomers and changes** (such as the reforming of the group for the next project).

(v) **Group cohesion is often intensified by inter-group competition,** which can lead to a culture of competitiveness, hostility and political game-playing.

Attention will need to be given to focusing the group's energies on the project, welcoming feedback (including constructive criticism), and emphasising competition rather than competitiveness.

(e) **What do we mean by team success?**

(i) The meeting of **task objectives,** standards and targets: in other words, effective job performance on the project.

(ii) The **satisfaction of individual team members,** in the relationships, processes and performance of the team. This can be measured by expressed attitudes, as well as by signs such as low absenteeism, open communication and so on.

(iii) **Effective and efficient team functioning**: co-operation, the balanced exercising of roles, workload sharing, individual contribution, consensus decision-making, performance in the leader's absence and so on.

(iv) **Effective and efficient task functioning**: few interruptions to work flow, ideas generation and problem-solving, constructive feedback, client focus and so on.

(v) The **fulfilment of the team's role** within the organisation: projecting a positive image of the organisation, reflecting organisational values, commitment to organisational goals.

12   INDIVIDUAL BEHAVIOUR

> **Tutor's hint.** This is quite a challenging question. Start by defining personality and attitudes, to anchor your answer in specifics. So much emphasis is placed, these days, on teamworking, that it is easy to forget that teams are not always the most suitable option. Part (b) invites you to consider when an individual might function more effectively on his or her own than in a team: think about your own experiences in group decision-making to give you some ideas.

(a) **Personality and work behaviour**

Personality is the total pattern of characteristic ways of thinking, feeling and behaving that constitute the individual's distinctive method of relating to the environment.

If our personality factors affect work behaviour

(i) **Different personality types may suit different types of work.** A person who is inhibited and introverted, for example, may find sales work, involving a lot of social interactions, intensely stressful – and will probably not be very effective.

(ii) **Different personality types may suit different organisational structures, systems and cultures.** Some people hate to be controlled, for example, while others prefer to work in bureaucratic organisations because they prefer the security, predictability and lack of individual responsibility.

(iii) Different personality types may 'clash' with each other: a prime source of conflict at work. Perfectionist personalities, for example, may be irritated by more 'laid back' characters (and vice versa).

(iv) **Different personality types will have different orientations to work.** Some people will be achievement- or results-oriented, while others will see work primarily as an opportunity for social interaction, satisfying activity, security or the earning of rewards. This will influence the effectiveness of the organisation's strategies for motivation.

Attitudes and work behaviour

Attitudes are mental states (comprised of beliefs, perceptions, feelings, desires and volition) which **predispose individuals** to behave in certain ways in certain contexts. Attitudes may affect work behaviour in the following ways.

(i) **Attitudes to work may be positive or negative**. These will include attitudes to working (as opposed to leisure), work colleagues, working conditions, the task, management, the organisation and so on. They will influence a wide variety of work behaviours: the extent of co-operation or conflict between individuals and groups or between workers and management; the extent of the employees commitment to and contribution to organisational goals; the kinds of incentives and rewards that will motivate the individual and so on.

(ii) **Individuals bring all sorts of attitudes about the world to work with them**. These may be attitudes to politics, education, religion, race and so on. They will affect how the individual relates to work colleagues, areas of agreement and conflict, shared perceptions or barriers to communication. Some attitudes may be specifically controlled in the workplace (through legislation and policy on sexual harassment, racial discrimination and so on).

(b) **Individual and group contribution**

Group working has certain advantages for task performance and worker satisfaction: the pooling of skills and resources; opportunities for social interaction; encouraging co-ordination and communication and so on.

However, groups are not always more effective than individual contribution.

(i) Individuals can **make decisions faster than groups** (although not always with the same amount of information and the same degree of acceptability).

(ii) Individuals **can focus on the task**, where groups give energy to relationships, conflicts and group maintenance.

(iii) Individuals can **exercise personal creativity** and flair, where group norms may encourage conformity.

(iv) Individuals are **more cautious in exercising responsibility**, where the shared responsibility in a group can lead to complacent and risky decisions.

13 ROLES AND PERCEPTIONS

> **Tutor's hint.** This may seem like a minor syllabus topic – but it is in the syllabus, so you need to be prepared. This is an example of the kind of detailed question that may be set. It is also an example of a highly structured question. Get used to allocating your time to reflect the marks available for each part of a question: two minutes per mark maximum!
>
> *Note* The format on part (b). You were asked to develop guidelines.

(a) **Definitions**

Perception is the psychological process by which stimuli (in-coming sensory data) are selected and organised into patterns which are meaningful to the individual. This includes two basic processes: **perceptual selection**, or the gathering and filtering of relevant data, and **perceptual organisation**, or the recognition and interpretation of

38

data. The essence of perception is that people see things differently: we respond not to the territory, but to the map – the picture we form of the world.

Roles are the parts people act out in different contexts, according to the tasks and relationships required by those contexts. A person may occupy a number of roles: as a worker (in the office); as a friend (with his peers); as a father (with his kids); as an enthusiast (at the golf club) and so on. The people who relate to a particular person in a particular role are called a *role set* and the signals given to show which role a person is in are called *role signs*.

(b) **Dealing with different perceptions**

Guidelines for staff

We don't respond to the world as it really is: we respond to the way we perceive it to be. And we all see things differently. This doesn't mean that we can't get on together, if we remember a few simple points.

(i) In the event of conflict or misunderstanding with a work colleague, consider carefully whether:

- You might be misinterpreting the situation
- They might be interpreting the situation differently from you

(ii) Try and see an issue or problem from the other person's point of view.

(iii) Don't confuse the map with the territory: recognise when 'right' and 'wrong' are merely matters of interpretation.

(iv) When tackling a task or problem, get the people involved to define the situation as they see it: negotiate a definition that can be shared.

(v) Be aware of the most common clashes of perception at work:

- 'Us and them': the experience of work can be very different for managers and staff, or for different departments
- Race and sex: be aware that jokes, comments and gestures that you find amusing may be offensive and discriminatory to someone else

---

(c) **Roles and relationships**

Roles define relationships, because they define the behaviours expected of a person in relation to other people in a given context. Roles affect work relationships in the following ways.

(i) The **'role set'** will determine the nature of the relationship between people within it. At work, relationships are defined by role sets based on the hierarchy of authority: your role as subordinate, for example, may define your relationship with your boss as professional, formal and respectful (depending on cultural norms in the organisation).

(ii) The **'role signs'** you give (indicating which 'hat' you have on) will define the relationship. Outside work, for example, you may be friends with your subordinates: at work, a more formal manner and task focus will signal the professional relationship.

(iii) People select relationships which provide **'role models'**: examples of how a person in that role should behave.

(iv) **'Role ambiguity'** or **'role incompatibility'** can complicate relationships by placing conflicting demands: it is difficult for a person to be both a friend and a boss, for example, in a disciplinary situation.

14   AUTHORITY AND POWER

> **Tutor's hint.** The introduction to the question sets up the important premise that there is a difference between authority and power and the sources of each in an organisational context: that is, authority is delegated by position in the organisation, while power is conferred by the leader's followers. In fact, the lines are not so clear cut: you may have recognised the opportunity to discuss line, staff and functional authority in part (b), as well as the 'types of power' classifications popularised by Charles Handy in part (c).

(a)   **Managerial authority and leadership power**

Authority is the right to do something. In an organisation, it refers to the scope and amount of discretion given to a manager to make decisions, by virtue of the position which the manager holds in the organisation.

Power is the ability to direct or modify the behaviour or attitudes of another person: the ability to influence. Power is not the same as authority. A manager may have the right to expect subordinates to carry out instructions, but may lack the ability to make them do so. On the other hand, an individual may have the ability to make others act in a certain way, without having the organisational authority to do so. Informal 'leaders' may be in this position.

(b)   **From where do managers derive their authority?**

A manager is appointed to a position of authority within the organisation. 'Line authority' is normally conferred or delegated from the top down, because managers can pass on some of their authority to subordinates in assigning tasks to them. (However, authority can also be bestowed from below, when it is conferred on a leader figure by people at lower levels in the hierarchy: elected trade union officials have this kind of authority.)

A manager's authority is mostly, therefore, a function of the position he or she holds. However, the term 'staff authority' is given to influence exercised by virtue of specialist skills or knowledge: for example, when an HR manager advises an Accounts manager on recruitment issues. This may also be recognised as 'functional authority', by which a manager is given formal authority to make or influence decisions in other departments by virtue of specialist skills or knowledge.

(c)   **From where do leaders derive their power?**

(i)   **Personal (or referent) power** is derived from the popularity or charisma of the individual.

(ii)   **Expert power** is derived from special expertise, skill or knowledge which is recognised and valued by others.

(iii)   **Physical or coercive power** is the power of superior force: this should not be prevalent in organisations, but may manifest itself in physical intimidation in some cultures (eg the armed forces).

(iv)   **Resource power** derives from the control over resources which are valued by others: a leader's ability to award or withhold pay, for example, to share information or to mobilise labour resources.

(v)   **Negative power** derives from the potential to cause trouble, hinder or sabotage the plans of others: for example, workers' power to withdraw their labour, or a leader's ability to leave the organisation taking client good will with him.

Whichever the type of power, **the essence of leadership is that it is conferred or made effective by followers.** 'It is the willingness of people to follow that makes a person a leader' (Koontz, O'Donnell, Weihrich). Leaders' power may be removed if their followers cease to acknowledge it.

15   AUTHORITY AND RESPONSIBILITY

> **Tutor's hint.** The introduction to this question gives you a guideline for your answer. Authority without responsibility means that authority can be exercised in an irresponsible way. Responsibility without authority is frustrating and stressful, because the person is accountable for events over which he has no control. This is an unstructured question, which you may find harder to plan than a structured one: start by defining your terms, and ensure that you include sufficient content to warrant 15 marks.

Delegated authority is a person's formal right to perform tasks and make decisions, which is passed down the scalar chain of command. **Responsibility is the level of performance and results for which that person is formally accountable** to his superiors.

A mismatch between the two would be defined as a situation where an individual has authority which exceeds his responsibility (that is, he is allowed to do things without being called to account for the results) or has responsibility without authority (that is, he is called to account for events over which he has no effective control).

If the formal organisation structure fails to make responsibility commensurate with authority (and vice versa) there will be **two main effects**.

(a)   **Managers not held accountable** for their authority may exercise that authority in a **capricious or irresponsible way,** which will not necessarily be to the benefit of the organisation. Even if they have the best interests of the organisation at heart, they may take unacceptable risks, because the consequences of decisions will not rebound on them.

(b)   Managers who are held accountable for aspects of performance which they have no authority to control are placed in an impossible situation and will become frustrated, stressed, demoralised and demotivated. Performance (and hence, potentially, that of the team) is likely to suffer.

There will also be spin-off effects.

(c)   **The organisation will fail to learn from its mistakes if accountability fails to operate effectively.** If a superior has delegated authority to a subordinate but fails to make him accountable, the superior will (rightly) be made responsible for any problems arising from the subordinate's errors of judgement – but the problem will not necessarily be effectively analysed and solved. The control mechanisms of the organisation depend on accountability.

(d)   If a superior does not give a subordinate enough **authority** to do a job, and the subordinate holds him accountable for failure to do the job properly, there is likely to be conflict. There will thus be two problems: likely failure in the task (because of inadequate resources to complete it effectively) and an on-going lack of co-operation, trust and respect in the work team.

(e)   **The management style 'leave alone and zap' has found to be a major cause of work stress,** and such a style may be reflected in a failure to delegate adequate authority ('leave alone') followed by holding the subordinate to account ('zap').

(f)   **Subordinates may complain that they have insufficient authority** to perform the tasks for which they are responsible, but this may be based on misperceptions. Subordinates may be demanding an impracticable degree of autonomy, or may

41

misunderstand the nature of delegation. They may also 'feel' more responsible for results than their actually accountabilities indicate. Subordinates may not understand the extent to which work depends on co-ordination with other departments: final authority over a project may lie outside the department and not be within the power of the manager to delegate. The consequences of a perceived mismatch of authority and responsibility might therefore be a lack of co-ordination, inter-departmental territorial disputes and unofficial empire building.

16   ENCOURAGING DELEGATION

> **Tutor's hint.** The introduction to the question sets you up with an answer to part (a). Note that only three marks are available for this part: resist the temptation to explain the reasons for delegation at excessive length. Reluctance to delegate should be fairly straightforward: think about why a manager might not trust subordinates (with and without good reason), and how an organisation might make the decision to delegate seem more or less risky.

(a) **Why is delegation necessary?**

(i)   There are **physical and mental limitations** to the workload and span of control of any individual or group in authority.

(ii) Managers and supervisors need to be freed **to concentrate on the higher-level aspects** of work which are their special responsibility (eg planning and control).

(iii) There are significant benefits for flexibility, quality and competitive advantage in delegating authority to front-line teams – particularly since highly skilled workers may expect such involvement in decisions affecting their work, and delegation will be an important tool in attracting and retaining staff.

(iv) Delegation trains staff for management succession.

(b) **Why are managers reluctant to delegate?**

(i)   **Low confidence** and trust in abilities of their staff, which may or may not be justified, especially given the burden of accountability for subordinates' mistakes.

(ii) A desire to **'stay in touch' with the team** – both in terms of workload and personal relationships – particularly if the manager is new in the management role.

(iii) Feeling **threatened** with redundancy by the abilities of subordinates and the perception that they could do the superior's job.

(iv) **Poor control and communication** systems in the organisation, so that the manager feels he has to do everything himself in order to retain any real control over events or to stay 'in the loop' for information.

(v)   An **organisation culture that fails to reward or recognise effective delegation,** so that the manager may not realise that delegation is a positive value (as opposed to shirking responsibility or losing control).

(vi) **Lack of education and training in delegation skills:** what it involves, how to do it effectively and so on. Managers may associate delegation with loss of control, making themselves redundant and so on.

(vii) Lack of **time management skills**, assertiveness skills and so on that enable a manager to delegate effectively.

(c) **Overcoming reluctance to delegate**

  (i)   **Train** the subordinates so that they are capable of handling delegated authority in a responsible way.

  (ii)   **Establish effective monitoring and control** systems that will reassure the superior that delegated authority is being exercised without risk.

  (iii)   **Improve communication systems**, especially upwards, so that superiors do not feel they are 'out of the loop' once whey have delegated authority to subordinates.

  (iv)   **Train superiors in delegation**, time management and assertiveness skills so that they are better able to prioritise their work and delegate work with confidence.

  (v)   **Create a culture which supports delegation:** articulating trust, recognising and rewarding delegation, backing up delegation with resources and structures that enable subordinates to fulfil delegated tasks and so on.

17   THE PURPOSE OF OBJECTIVE SETTING

> **Tutor's hint.** This is another highly structured question, so your answers to the various parts can be brief – but time management may be an issue: you will need to use your prioritising and summarising skills. Part (a) allows you to distinguish between qualitative 'aims' and quantifiable 'objectives': resist the temptation to write about SMART objectives, which is not strictly relevant. Parts (b) and (c) ask you to distinguish between the benefits of objective-setting to the organisation and the effects of objective-setting on individual behaviour: motivation, learning and so on. Part (d) offers wide scope for specific answers: ours are suggestions only.

(a) **Objectives**

Objectives are operational, quantitative goals: desired results or outcomes which can be expressed in quantitative or numerical terms. Objectives can thus be distinguished from 'aims', which are non-operational, qualitative goals. There is likely to be a hierarchy of objectives, with a primary corporate objective (in business, usually profitability) and secondary or subordinate objectives (in areas such as market share or position, product development and so on).

(b) **Organisational purposes of objective-setting**

Objectives focus the energies of the organisation on its priorities for survival and prosperity. Objectives enable management to:

  (i)   Implement the corporate mission, by outlining what needs to be achieved

  (ii)   Publicise the direction and goals of the organisation to managers, staff and other stakeholders, so that they know where their efforts should be directed and how their own interests can be integrated with those of the organisation

  (iii)   Appraise the validity of strategic decisions, by assessing their effectiveness in achieving stated objectives

  (iv)   Assess and control actual performance, as objectives can be used as targets and yardsticks of achievement

(c) **Behavioural purposes of setting objectives**

People are 'purposive': they act in pursuit of particular goals. Goals or objectives influence what we perceive (because we filter out anything that is irrelevant to our goals), what we learn (because we modify our behaviour in order to meet our goals more effectively in future) and what we do (because we are motivated to behave in ways that meet our goals). Clear objectives help individuals to:

(i)   Plan and direct their effort towards those objectives

(ii)   Monitor their performance against objectives and adjust (learn) where required

(iii)   Experience the reward of achievement, once objectives have been reached

(iv)   Feel that their tasks have meaning and purpose, an important element in job satisfaction

(v)   Experience the incentive (motivation) of a challenge: the need to expend energy and effort in a particular direction in order to achieve something

(vi)   Avoid the de-motivation of impossible, unclear or inadequately rewarded tasks

(d) **Examples of organisational objectives**

- Specific targets for profitability, return on capital employed or earnings per share

- Specific targets for market share or growth in market share

- Specific targets for product development, investment in research and development or innovation

- Specific targets for productivity, reductions in the cost per unit of output or quality improvements

- Specific targets for human resource utilisation and development, increases in employee retention or skill levels

18   SOCIAL RESPONSIBILITY

> **Tutor's hint.** This is a provocative question. The concept of 'enlightened self interest' is based on Friedman's assertion that the only responsibility of a business organisation (as opposed to a public sector one) is profit maximisation for the wealth of its owners over the long term. Business organisations do not have the luxury of being 'enlightened' purely for the sake of society, although they recognise society as stakeholders in the business. This argument underpins part (a): beware of citing social responsibility as a Good Thing in purely ideological terms, however you feel about it. Part (b) offers the opportunity to list many possible areas of concern and interest, of which our suggestions are only a sample: make sure that you include some specifically ethical objectives (such as eliminating bribery) as well as socially responsible ones (such as environmental conservation).

(a) **Business benefits of social responsibility**

Socially responsible policies benefit the business in the following ways.

(i)   Employee benefits over the statutory minimum may aid **the organisation in attracting, motivating and retaining high-quality staff,** particularly in times of competition for scarce skills.

(ii)   Social responsibility reflects fashionable issues of concern among consumer and labour groups. Policies may be part of:

- The **product/service brand** of the organisation, attracting the trust and support (and therefore business) of like-minded consumers (as, for example, in the case of The Body Shop) and investors

- The **employer brand** of the organisation, positioning it as an ethical, trustworthy and people-friendly employer, enabling it to attract and retain skilled labour

(iii) Offering customer benefits, added value or quality may be perceived as socially responsible, but is also a powerful source of **customer loyalty**. Retaining customers, and gaining their repeat business, is far more cost effective than winning new customers.

(iv) **Sponsorship may also be perceived as socially responsible** in supporting the cultural, sporting or educational life of the community, but it is also an opportunity to raise brand awareness and exercise public relations activities.

(v) Sustainable economic and environmental practices are **investments in the prosperity of the business,** protecting working relationships, resource and investment streams over the long term.

(b) **Areas for socially responsible and ethical objectives**

Social responsibility

- Environmental impact study, waste management, ecology and conservation and so on

- Product labelling, compensation to customers under Fair Trading legislation and so on

- Health, safety, welfare, employment protection and consultation provisions for staff

- Donations, sponsorships and staff secondments to charitable and community causes

- Supporting suppliers (especially in developing countries)

Business ethics

- Treatment of women, ethnic minorities and other disadvantaged groups in employment

- Sustainable and ethical business and investment practices overseas (not exploiting cheap labour or resources, not investing in illegal or unethical businesses)

- Policies on bribes, transparency and disclosure of conflicts of interest

- Ethical contracts management (tendering, exploitation of contract labour)

The Body Shop and Johnson & Johnson are two examples of businesses which have positioned themselves as ethical leaders in their markets.

19   PERFORMANCE MANAGEMENT

> **Tutor's hint.** The introduction to the question should indicate what is meant by performance management: not 'people management' in general, not merely 'appraisal'. This should make part (a) fairly straightforward. You may have had to think more carefully about part (b): we have answered it with a generally applicable planning hierarchy. You may prefer to use a competence or Management By Objectives framework.

(a) **Performance management**

Performance management 'is a process to establish a shared understanding about what is to be achieved, and an approach to managing and developing people... [so that it] will be achieved.' The process is as follows.

45

Step 1 From the business plan, **identify the requirements and competencies** required to fulfil corporate objectives.

Step 2 Draw up a **performance agreement,** defining what is expected of the individual or team, covering standards of performance, performance indicators and the skills and competencies people require.

Step 3 **Draw up a performance and development plan**, in collaboration with the individual or team, which outlines the actions needed to improve performance to the levels outlined in the performance agreement. Discussions will typically cover:

- The areas of performance in which the individual feels in need of development

- Identified problems or shortfalls and agreed measures and targets for improvement

- Opportunities for training and development

Step 4 **Monitor, feed back and adjust performance** on an on-going basis, in order to:

- Update work plans as required
- Recognise and reward performance that meets or exceeds target
- Deal with performance problems and shortfalls
- Identify continual improvement and development opportunities

Step 5 Review performance annually, in an on-going cycle

(b) **Determining goals, standards and competence requirements**

The following is a basic hierarchical framework for determining specific goals, standards and competence requirements that dovetail with the hierarchy of objectives of the organisation, for use in performance management.

Step 1 Set unit objectives for all teams or departments, in terms of primary targets: for example, relating to the achievement of production schedules, output quality or resource utilisation.

Step 2 Set secondary or sub-targets for each of these primary targets.

Step 3 Analyse the targets as a series of **key results** (objectives which must be achieved for the improvement targets to be achieved) and **key tasks** (things that must be done on time and to the required standard if the key results are to be achieved).

Step 4 Determine **performance standards**: definitions of how well key tasks must be performed in order to achieve key results.

Step 5 Establish **specific short-term goals** for key tasks, against which progress can be monitored.

Step 6 Formulate **action plans,** specifying 'what, how, who, when, where and how much' are required to reach short-term goals.

Within this process, there may be a wide range of specific performance criteria and measures, under the general headings of effectiveness, efficiency, economy, elegance and ethicality.

20   RECRUITMENT RESPONSIBILITIES

> **Tutor's hint.** This should be quite straightforward if you are familiar with the material. Questions about 'factors in a decision' generally refer to matters to be considered: for example, cost or time/speed. You could, arguably, answer with advantages and disadvantages, but they are more likely to be specified in the question if they are what the examiner expects to see.

(a)   **HR role in recruitment**

Some aspects of recruitment and selection are increasingly being devolved to the line managers who will be responsible for the performance of the recruits. However, in most organisations the HR department will retain responsibility for:

(i)   Assessing the organisations **human resource requirements** (human resource planning)

(ii)   **Monitoring the labour market,** skill availability and trends in recruitment media and methods

(iii)   **Formulating recruitment policies** in regard to such matters as internal recruitment, compliance with equal opportunities legislation, content of job advertisements and so on

(iv)   **Liaising with recruitment consultants**, careers offices and other on-going sources of labour and contacts;

(v)   **Job advertising** and **initial screening** of applicants.

The full extent of the involvement of the HR department will vary according to the seniority and specialism of the vacancy, the complexity of the job market for the position, organisational policies and procedures and so on.

(b)   **The role of recruitment consultants**

Recruitment consultants offer flexible menu of services to suit the varying needs of the organisation. Consultants may be retained to advise and recommend, or to carry out recruitment on behalf of the organisation. Some recruitment consultants specialise in particular grades and types of staff: for example, accountancy personnel. They can offer the following services.

(i)   Analysing, or taking **briefings** on, the organisation's labour requirements: vacancies, cultural preferences and so on.

(ii)   Helping to draw up, or offering **advice** on, job descriptions, person specifications, application forms and other recruitment tools.

(iii)   **Advertising vacancies** on behalf of the organisation.

(iv)   **Initial screening** of applications and short-listing of suitable candidates for interview.

(v)   Guidance or help with interviewing and selection testing.

(c)   **Factors in the decision of whether to use recruitment consultants**

(i)   The level of expertise and specialist knowledge which the consultant can bring to the recruitment process, and whether such skills are available within the organisation.

(ii)   Whether there is a need for impartiality (to avoid organisational 'cloning') or anonymity (to avoid competitor interest), which only an outsider to the organisation can offer.

(iii) Whether the structure and politics of the organisation support in-house or external decision-making: whether, for example, outsiders are regarded with suspicion, or encourage freer discussion of internal processes and problems.

(iv) The time it will take for consultants to learn about the job and the organisation in order to articulate requirements accurately, and whether urgency is a factor.

(v) The cost of employing consultants in relation to the benefits: if there is a plentiful pool of suitable skills, for example, specialist help may not be cost-effective.

21 JOB DESCRIPTION

> **Tutor's hint.** Note that this question is asked in the context of job redesign, not recruitment and selection: do not confine your comments on the usefulness of job descriptions to the recruitment process. You may have had to think in order to come up with drawbacks for part (b): think about the need for flexibility in organisations, and about multi-skilling, teamworking and 'jobless structures'...

(a) **Uses and benefits of job descriptions**

A **job description** is a written statement of those facts which are important in a job regarding the duties, responsibilities and their organisational and operational interrelationships.

Job descriptions are commonly used in the following circumstances.

(i) In **recruitment,** job descriptions:

- Define what skills and qualifications are required of the holder of the job described to assist in the formulation of person specifications and recruitment advertisements and during the interview/testing phase of selection.

- Define the requirements of the job as a means of determining rates of pay for the job holder, if this has not been done by other means.

- Ensure that the job will be a full-time and challenging job for the recruit and will not under-utilise his or her capacities.

(ii) In **job evaluation,** for establishing wage rates. Job descriptions offer a standardised format, making it easier to compare and grade jobs, and focusing attention on the job (not the job holder).

(iii) In **induction,** training, appraisal and development: to highlight the scope and functions of the job, training needs, lines of potential career development and so on.

(iv) **In organisation design and change management.** Job descriptions indicate the effectiveness of job design (the extent to which tasks are integrated, well distributed and so on) and organisation structure (lines of reporting, spans of control and so on).

(b) **Limitations and drawbacks of job descriptions**

(i) They are only suited for jobs where the work is **largely repetitive** and **predictable**: once the element of discretion and flexibility comes into a job, the job description will be at best irrelevant and at worst a straitjacket.

(ii) **Management jobs are likely to be constantly changing** as external influences impact upon them, so a job description is constantly out of date.

(iii) Difficulties arise when job descriptions are taken too **literally**, and cause **demarcation disputes**. People may adhere strictly to the contents of the job description, rather than responding flexibly to task or organisational requirements: this in turn can lead to costly over-manning practices.

(iv) In today's fast-changing environment, when responsiveness to customer demands is encouraging multi-skilling, horizontal structures and flexible working practices, it is arguable whether the 'job' as such is a relevant concept.

It must be remembered that a job description is a static 'snapshot' of a job at a given time: it requires flexibility and constant, negotiated revision. It must also be remembered that 'the map is not the territory': job descriptions are designed as a tool for management, not a constraint.

22   JOB ADVERTISEMENT

> **Tutor's hint.** Part (a) of this question is quite general and leaves you plenty of scope: try and spread your guidelines across issues of objectives, content, presentation and so on. Remember not to discuss media here, as this is the topic of part (b). Part (b) is an example of specific topic and instruction keywords. 'Evaluate' means critically appraising the good and bad points – not just listing or describing. 'Advertising media' gives you half the content key: 'relevant to this vacancy' (ie an accounts assistant) gives you the other.

(a)

GUIDELINES: EFFECTIVE JOB ADVERTISEMENT

The object of recruitment advertising is to attract suitable candidates and deter unsuitable candidates. The following are some of the basic points to bear in mind.

1. The advertisement needs to include job factors (based on the job description), person factors (based on the person specification) and organisation factors (based on corporate identity policies).

2. The advertisement should be concise, but sufficient to give a prospective candidate a meaningful indication of his or her suitability for the job and its suitability for him or her.

3. The advertisement needs to be attractive to the maximum number of suitable candidates: offering appropriate rewards, challenges and positive values for the type of person the organisation wishes to recruit.

4. The advertisement needs to be honest about the job and the organisation. Disappointed expectations will be a prime source of dissatisfaction when an applicant actually comes into contact with the organisation.

5. The advertisement needs to be relevant to the vacancy: specific skills, qualifications and aptitudes required should be prominently set out.

6. The advertisement should clearly specify how to apply, to whom and by what date.

7. The advertisement should be presented in line with corporate identity policies (in regard to logos, typestyles, cultural values and so on).

8. The advertisement should be formatted for, and transmitted by, appropriate advertising media, taking into account the nature of the job, the audience of the medium and the cost of advertising.

(b) **Relevant media options**

(i) The **in-house magazine, notice board and/or staff website.** This is an inexpensive option, and has the benefit of attracting candidates whose performance record is known, and who know how the organisation operates.

Considering these advantages, targeting is adequate: staff at other sites and in other sections of the organisation may well have accounting skills, or know someone (perhaps from their own accountancy studies) who does.

(ii) **Professional and specialist journals**, such as the ACCA's *Student Accountant* or *Accountancy Age*. These have the benefit of targeting a pre-selected audience, and are therefore cost-effective and efficient, despite taking in a geographically wider audience than may be strictly relevant to our needs.

(iii) The Employment Opportunities section of the corporate website offers a cost-effective way of attracting individuals who are technology-literate and already interested in the organisation. On-line advertising at Employment Search sites may be another option for access to a wider market, at greater cost.

(iv) The Accounting Jobs section of the local newspaper offers targeting on the basis of sector and geography, and need not be expensive (being local) for a small classified advertisement (perhaps pointing candidates to the web site for more information).

23   SCENARIO: SELECTION METHODS

> **Tutor's hint.** You should be able to diagnose FGH's problem from the scenario given, which will be useful for part (e) in particular. You should immediately spot a problem in the exclusive use of interviewing: not the most predictive of selection tools. In addition, you may note that the selection process seems to give both FGH and its recruits a false idea of their suitability for each other: hence the early departure of recruits and the larger-than-expected expenditure on training – presumably to bring recruits up to scratch. The questions rightly require a wholesale review of the selection process: giving you an opportunity to display wide-ranging knowledge in this area. Only part (e) requires analysis and problem-solving: think about some of the issues in selection not yet dealt with in other parts of the question…

(a) **Qualities of an effective job application form**

Part of FGH's selection problems may come from the ineffective gathering of application information from tools such as cvs and letters. Application forms can aid in weeding out unsuitable candidates and identifying potentially suitable candidates, if attention is given to the following factors.

(i) Questions asked should be **specific and relevant** to the requirements of the advertised vacancy. They should be designed with reference to the requirements set out in the person specification for the job (if available).

(ii) Questions should be **closed,** or options given, **where specific answers are required,** but **open**, with space provided, where the organisation wishes the **candidate to demonstrate his or her powers** of concise and orderly self-expression (eg giving reasons for wanting the job, describing key successes and failures).

(iii) The application form should be **easy to complete**: clear as to the type and method of answers required; not so time-consuming as to discourage careful completion; giving sufficient space for answers and so on.

(iv) The application form should **project a positive image** of the style and values of the organisation and confirm to corporate identity guidelines.

(v) Questions should be vetted for **compliance with equal opportunities and anti-discrimination legislation.**

(vi) Application forms should be formatted for use on-line (as well as in hard-copy form), with the advantages of computerised data capture and application processing.

(b) **Limitations of interviews**

Although no selection method offers 100% predictive validity, it is noticeable from research studies that although the most popular selection technique, interviews are very limited in their ability to predict job performance

(i) **Interviews are limited in scope**. They are too brief to allow the gathering of all the information required to predict the behaviour of the candidate in a variety of circumstances.

(ii) They are **artificial situations**, in which candidates are likely to be highly prepared and rehearsed, on their best behaviour and/or highly nervous.

(iii) They are limited in relevance, in that they **are not able to assess job-relevant factors** such as 'the candidate's ability to get on with and influence his colleagues, to display qualities of spontaneous leadership and to produce ideas in a real-life situation' (Plumbley).

(iv) **Errors of perception and judgement** may be made by interviewers, including various forms of bias, stereotyping and generalisation, poor use of criteria and the subjective perception of qualitative factors such as 'integrity' or 'motivation'.

(v) **Lack of skill or experience in interviewers** may result in poor interview planning and direction, and failure to probe beneath the surface of pre-prepared answers.

(vi) **Interviewers may fail to give sufficient or sufficiently relevant information** to candidates to allow them to judge their own suitability for the job or organisation (as is suggested by the early departure of FGH's recruits).

(c) **A range of other selection techniques**

A wide range of alternative or supplementary techniques is available, and may be more or less appropriate depending on the nature of the vacancy.

(i) **Selection testing methods** include:

- **Intelligence or IQ** testing (which can be broadened to include different types of intelligence, including practical, mechanical, emotional and so on)

- **Aptitude and proficiency** testing in specific skill attainment. (In the case of the Payroll Assistant, for example, a simple in-tray exercise using the firm's payroll software might be used)

- **Psychometric or personality** testing, if FGH can develop a relevant framework of criteria for assessment

- Case studies and 'in-tray' exercises to simulate work situations and problems

(ii) **Group selection methods** or assessment centres: generally used for managerial positions. Group selections require specialist facilitation and interpretation, using role plays, case studies, leaderless discussion groups and so on to display candidates' leadership, interpersonal and problem-solving skills.

(iii) **Work sampling**: perusal of the candidate's portfolio, or setting work exercises.

(iv) **Biodata questionnaires**: scoring candidates according to biographical data which has been found to correlate with successful job performance in comparable positions.

      (v)   **Reference and background checks** (discussed further below), to confirm details provided in the course of the application and to get third-party assessment of the candidate's employability (although the objectivity of the source may be an issue).

Still other methods, such as graphology, cannot be recommended as offering any advantage for predictive validity. It is recommended that a mix of relevant techniques be used for each vacancy, in order to maximise the reliability of selection data gathered.

(d)   **Information in references**

      (i)   **Factual information to confirm assertions** made by the candidate in regard to previous employment, qualifications, circumstances of leaving and so on. This information is material in confirming the integrity of the candidate, as well as useful detail about his or her abilities and motivations.

      (ii)   **Opinions about the applicant's personality and other attributes**. These should be treated with some caution: allowance should be made for prejudice (favourable or unfavourable), charity (withholding detrimental remarks) and fear of being actionable for defamation.

      (iii) **Assessment as to the employability of the candidate**. Again, treated with caution as subjective, the question 'would you re-employ this individual?' (asked of a previous employer) may be a valuable guide for the recruiting organisation.

(e)   **Other recommendations**

FGH clearly has a problem in retaining its new recruits. There appear to be particular issues with **post induction crisis** (recruits failing to settle in to the organisation once employed), **unrealistic expectations by recruits** (resulting in disappointment with the experience of employment) and **unrealistic expectations by FGH** (resulting in unexpected needs for training and development). In addition to the matters discussed above, the following measures may be recommended.

      (i)   **Reviewing job advertising** (and other recruitment and selection messages) to ensure that expectations raised are realistic in relation to the actual experience and rewards offered by the job.

      (ii)   **Reviewing job descriptions and person specifications** to ensure that the criteria for selection are sufficiently stringent and relevant to the job. It may be that our stated requirements for qualifications, skills and experience are insufficient for effective job performance: hence the need to train new recruits.

      (iii) **Implementing more thorough, relevant and on-going induction programmes**, so that recruits are helped to fit in to the social structure and culture of FGH, provided with support networks (eg mentors) and supported in identifying initial training and coaching needs. This may minimise the subsequent post-induction crisis.

      (iv) **Monitoring and reviewing the recruitment and selection** process on an on-going basis, to evaluate the predictive success of selection methods, monitor the progress of new recruits and so on *before* major problems arise.

Additional recommendations may include: 'trial periods' or renewable contracts, exit interviews with leaving recruits to identify specific problems and considering the use of specialist recruitment and selection consultants.

24   INTERVIEWS

> **Tutor's hint.** Most firms use the interview as their main tool for selection decisions – but it is one of the least effective predictors of future job performance. This is obviously not an argument for abolishing interviews, but for learning to use them more effectively. You may interpret part (b) as an opportunity to discuss the potential pitfalls in interviewing and how to overcome them. We have chosen a more general discussion of 'factors' such as preparation, questioning styles, listening and so on.

(a)   **Purposes of selection interviews**

    (i)   **Finding the best person** for the job, by giving the organisation a chance to assess applicants (and particularly their interpersonal communication skills) directly.

    (ii)   **Marking sure that applicants understand** what the job entails and offers and whether the organisation will satisfy their employment objectives.

    (iii)   **Giving a positive impression** of the organisation, both to persuade chosen candidates to accept the job offer and to create a positive employer brand in the labour market.

    (iv)   Ensuring that all applicants feel that they have been **fairly treated,** both for positive employer branding and compliance with equal opportunities law.

(b)   **Factors in effective interviewing**

    (i)   The interview should be conducted in the light **of consistent, specific, measurable, performance-relevant criteria,** set out in job descriptions, person specifications or competency profiles.

    (ii)   Criteria such as interpersonal communication skills, rapport-building and on-the-spot analysis and problem-solving should be directly monitored during the interview. Case studies and other tests could be used to demonstrate other job-relevant skills.

    (iii)   The interview should be conducted in such a way as to minimise the artificial and stressful dynamics of the situation.

    (iv)   Interviewers should be trained in **effective interviewing techniques,** including:

- Pacing and controlling the interview
- Building (and standing back from) rapport and empathy with the candidate
- Using appropriate questioning styles for specific purposes
- Listening actively to surface content and non-verbal subtexts
- Avoiding all forms of direct and indirect discrimination

    (v)   **Remaining elements of bias should be controlled** by cross-checking assessments with other interviewers or other selection techniques (eg testing)

    (vi)   **Sufficient time and resources** should be allocated to interviews so that they are (and are seen to be) conducted purposefully and fairly.

    (vii)   **Candidates must be given the opportunity to seek and clarify any information** they need about the job and the organisation.

    (viii)   The process should be monitored and appraised in the light of successful candidates' performance.

25   EVALUATING RECRUITMENT AND SELECTION

> **Tutor's hint.** The instruction keywords are important here, distinguishing between 'four methods of evaluating' (monitoring the workforce, using attitude surveys and so on) in part (a) and 'seven criteria for evaluating' (cost-effectiveness of advertising, meeting equal opportunity targets, generating suitable applications and so on) in part (b). A wide range of specific performance indicators could have been given in part (b): note that you only need to list seven to earn the marks.

(a)   **Methods of evaluation**

    (i)   **Monitoring the composition of, and changes in, the workforce**

        For example, the proportion of women or ethnic minorities in the workforce might indicate effective or ineffective practice in the light of equal opportunities policies. The labour retention (or turnover) rates among new recruits might indicate effective or ineffective management of the expectations of recruits.

    (ii)   **Monitoring the job performance and development of successful recruits**

        Expectations and predictions made on the basis of interviews and selection testing can be compared to actual job performance, to indicate where criteria are more or less relevant and predictive, or where assessment has been inaccurate.

    (iii)   **Using attitude surveys and feedback questionnaires**

        The organisation can gather qualitative data in order to analyse successful and unsuccessful candidates' experience and perceptions of the recruitment and selection process. This may highlight areas of perceived unfairness, poor public relations, unnecessary stress and so on.

    (iv)   **Monitoring the effectiveness of recruitment policies,** campaigns, methods and media according to specific performance indicators (discussed below).

        For example: the organisation may analyse the cost effectiveness of different recruitment advertising media, defined as the cost per applicant, or cost per applicant short-listed for interview.

(b)   **Performance indicators for evaluating recruitment and selection**

- Number of candidates attracted

- Number of suitable candidates attracted (eg number or proportion of candidates who proceeded to interview or short-list)

- Number of women, ethnic minorities or disabled people attracted and selected, in relation to relevant policies and targets

- Cost of recruitment and selection per suitable (short-listed) candidate or successful candidate

- Cost-effectiveness of each advertising medium or selection method used (for comparison)

- Average time taken to process applications, or time taken for the whole process from job requisition to employment

- Post-selection performance of successful candidates in terms of meeting performance or development targets

- Number or proportion of recruits still employed after one year, two years

26 AREAS OF DISCRIMINATION

> **Tutor's hint.** Since the introduction noted the widening range of discrimination issues, you need to cover a fair amount of ground in your answer to part (a). In the UK, you should ensure that you have discussed not just gender, race and disability but spent convictions, sexual orientation, pregnancy, trade union membership and age. (The advantage of such a wide-ranging answer is that you do not have to say too much about each in order to earn the ten marks available!) Remember to answer in regard to a country of your choice: use your own local knowledge.

(a) **Areas of discrimination**

UK law and regulation (now partly based on the provisions of EU directives) covers discrimination in the following areas.

   (i) **Sex** (including marital status and change of sex) are covered by the Sex Discrimination Act and related regulations, which outlaw discrimination in all aspects of employment: recruitment and selection, access to training and promotion, redundancy and dismissal, access to pension facilities, retirement ages and so on.

   The Equal Pay Act 1970 and related regulations also cover the rights of women to equal pay for 'work of equal value' in relation to men.

   There are also legal provisions on gender-related issues such as pregnancy and equal treatment for part-time and temporary workers (most of whom are women).

   (ii) **Race and ethnic origin.** The Race Relations Act outlaws most types of discrimination on the grounds of colour, race, nationality and ethnic or national origin.

   (iii) Disability is covered by the **Disability Discrimination Act 1995**, which contains provisions for disabled access employment opportunities. Disability is defined as physical or mental impairment that has a substantial and long-term adverse effect on a person's ability to carry out normal day-to-day activities.

   (iv) The **Rehabilitation of Offenders Act** allows employees and job candidates to refuse to disclose previous ('spent') convictions for certain offences.

   (v) The right to trade union membership and activities (actual or proposed) or refusal to join a trade union are protected under the Employment Rights Act 1996.

   (vi) **Sexual orientation** is due to be covered by EU directive (Article 13) by 2003.

   (vii) **Age discrimination** is currently self-regulated under a voluntary Code of Practice on Age Diversity in Employment, Article 13 provisions on age are due to be enacted in UK law by 2006.

(b) **Direct and indirect discrimination**

Direct discrimination occurs when one interested group is treated less favourably than another (except for specifically exempted reasons), for example by an organisation's advertising for staff of a particular gender or ethnic origin. It is unlikely that a prospective employer will practise direct discrimination unawares.

Indirect discrimination occurs when requirements or conditions are imposed, with which a substantial proportion of the interested group could not comply, to their detriment. For example, the requirement that 'all applicants must work evenings and weekends' would restrict more women than men because of family responsibilities. The employer must, if challenged, justify the conditions on non-racial or non-sexual grounds. It is often claimed that employers are not aware that they are discriminating in this way.

27 MANAGING DIVERSITY

> **Tutor's hint.** This question covers issues you may not have encountered previously: ensure that you understand the points raised in our solution. Essentially, diversity covers a much wider appreciation of the ways in which people differ than equal opportunities provisions.

(a) **Managing diversity**

The concept of managing diversity is based on the belief that the individual differences we currently focus on under equal opportunities (gender, race, age and so on) are crude and irrelevant classifications of the most obvious differences between people, and should be replaced by a genuine understanding of the ways in which individuals differ.

The ways in which people are meaningfully different in the workplace include personality, preferred working style and individual needs and expectations. These things do not necessarily correlate with racial or gender differences in any way. For example, it would be a gross oversimplification to say that all women in an organisation require assertiveness training: it may be less appropriate for many women than for some men.

Thus, **effective managers seek to understand the job-relevant ways in which their staff differ,** and should seek to manage their performance in ways which recognise those differences as far as possible. Managers need to understand the unique contribution each person – not each 'category of person' – can make to the team.

A 'managing diversity' orientation implies the need to be proactive in managing the needs of a diverse workforce in areas (beyond equal opportunity and discrimination) such as:

- Tolerance of individual differences

- Communicating effectively with (and motivating) ethnically diverse workforces

- Managing workers with diverse family structures and responsibilities

- Managing the adjustments to be made by the ageing workforce

- Managing diverse career aspirations and paths

- Confronting literacy, numeracy and qualifications issues in an international workforce

- Managing co-operative working in diverse teams

(b) **Ways of creating and supporting diversity at work**

US multi-national Pitney Bowes has formulated an award-winning strategic plan on diversity, comprising the following five goals.

(i) **Communications**: 'Our vision of diversity and its implications for the organisation will be clearly communicated to all of us'

(ii) **Education and training**: 'We will become sensitive to and demonstrate an understanding of the value of differences through education and training'

(iii) **Career development**: 'We will create a culture that enables and encourages the development and upward mobility of all of us'

(iv) **Recruitment and hiring**: 'We will further increase the diversity of our employees so that our organisation reflects the demographic changes in our labour force'

(v) **Work/life balance**: 'We will provide a flexible and supportive work environment for employees in achieving a balance of work/life issues'

28   EFFECTIVE EQUAL OPPORTUNITIES POLICY

> **Tutor's hint.**   Note that part (a) asks for a planning/implementation process - 'a five-step plan' – not a set of recommendations for specific positive action initiatives (which is the subject of part (b)). In other words, how would an organisation go about putting meaningful equal opportunities policies in place?

(a) **Five-step plan to implement equal opportunities**

The following stages are necessary in order to create both the cultural support and policy framework for equal opportunities.

Step 1 **Secure support from the top of the organisation** for the formulation and implementation of practical policies. If necessary, senior accountabilities for equal opportunities may have to be created: for example, by appointing an Equal Opportunities Manager.

Step 2 **Set up a working party**, drawn from (for example) management, trade unions or staff associations, minority groups represented in the workforce, the HR function and staff representatives. This group's brief will be to produce a draft Policy and Code of Practice which will be approved at senior level.

Step 3 **Formulate action plans and allocate resources** (including staff) to implement and monitor the policy, publicise it to staff and other stakeholders, arrange training and counselling and so on.

Step 4 **Implement monitoring and review systems.** The numbers of women, ethnic minority and disabled staff, for example, can easily be monitored:

- On entering (or applying to enter) the organisation during recruitment
- On leaving the organisation
- On applying for transfers, promotions, training programmes and so on.

Step 5 **Plan and implement positive action initiatives** (discussed further below): taking active steps to encourage people from disadvantaged groups to apply for jobs and training and to compete for opportunities. (Note that this is not defined as 'positive discrimination'.)

(b) **Specific positive action measures**

(i) Using **ethnic languages** in job advertisements to facilitate applications from people of non-English-speaking background.

(ii) **Offering flexible hours**, part-time working, term-time or annual hours contracts (allowing for school holidays) to help women to combine careers with family responsibilities, with comparable terms to standard-contract workers. (Other measures friendly to women include workplace childcare facilities, training for women returners, career-break schemes and so on).

(iii) **Alteration of premises** and equipment to accommodate wheelchair users, blind/partially-sighted and deaf workers.

(iv)   The **harmonisation of HR policies** and benefits for employees of a particular marital status and/or sexual orientation. For example, extension of 'spouse' benefits to same-sex partners, as at British Airways.

(v)   **Fast-tracking school-leavers** as well as graduates, and posting managerial vacancies internally, giving more opportunities for groups currently at lower levels of the organisational or educational ladder.

29   SCENARIO: TRAINING

> **Tutor's hint.** Although this scenario covers training and development, it also examines your skills at written communication: note that you are asked to provide your answer in draft report format, and that it will need to be a persuasive report in order to overcome your Manager's negative attitudes to training. This is a highly structured question with detailed topic and instruction key words: part (a) asks for benefits of training; part (b) asks for a method of identify training needs (not for training needs themselves); part (c) asks for recommendations on training methods and media (appropriate to the scenario); part (d) asks for a method of evaluating training; and part (e) for a definition of development (which is not just the same as training). Make sure you have answered all the questions as set!

REPORT: TRAINING AND DEVELOPMENT AT JIK LTD

Prepared by: Your Name, Assistant Store Manager
For: M Hlavcek, Store Manager
Purpose: To consider the implications of recent customer feedback surveys and the need for systematic staff training in order to retain customer loyalty and competitive edge.

I   THE BENEFITS OF TRAINING

Recent customer feedback has suggested that the levels of technical and product knowledge and customer service skills of our staff are:

(a)   Inadequate to meet customer expectations

(b)   Impacting on the satisfaction and loyalty of customers

While it is acknowledged that training is no substitute for strategic staff selection, and that it bears a cost in time and resources, training can bring the following significant benefits.

Benefits for the organisation	Benefits for the individual
Increased skills, knowledge and competence: enhanced job performance	Enhanced competence: sense of achievement, self-esteem and security
Continuous improvement of the skill base, and greater employee retention: adding value to the human assets of the business	Opportunities for greater contribution to customer satisfaction and business success, which are a source of job satisfaction
Enhanced workforce flexibility and potential for management succession	
Better customer service, leading to customer retention (which is more cost-effective than winning new customers)	Opportunities for increased rewards and career development
Fewer purchase returns, complaints, service queries and so on (which waste time and resources)	Opportunities to extend own interests and skills in photography
Less need for detailed staff supervision and managerial intervention in problems	Knock-on effects of training needs analysis: potential improvements in work methods, supervisory style and so on.

II IDENTIFYING TRAINING NEEDS

We do not propose that indescriminate training be given, with a waste of time and resources. Specific training needs, relevant to JIK's customer care and business requirements, could be identified as follows.

Training needs from the perspective of the organisation or store as a whole can be identified from the business plan and strategy. This should set out planned store expansions, areas of diversification (eg into digital photographic services) and so on. JIK should address the implications of strategies in a coherent human resources plan, which would have many spin-off benefits for the planning of recruitment, selection, development and so on.

Training needs analysis may be carried out on a store-by-store or individual-by-individual basis. Training needs may be identified by the following means.

(i) **Monitoring new products**, legislation and customer demands which may create new skill or knowledge gaps (for example, the introduction of digital cameras).

(ii) **Monitoring critical incidents** which affect a key area of the organisation's effectiveness, and which may require training: customer complaints have already been identified.

(iii) Employee **self-assessments** and attitude surveys: inviting staff to identify areas in which they feel their performance is suffering from skill or knowledge gaps. (Many of the staff readily admit ignorance of new products and are keen to learn, since this is their area of interest.)

(iv) **Comparing the current skills**, knowledge and competence of staff (as assessed by specific testing or our usual appraisal systems) with the skills, knowledge and competence requirements indicated by the human resource plan, job descriptions and – most importantly - customer feedback. The shortfall may be called the 'training gap'.

III METHODS OF TRAINING

Once specific training needs have been identified, and specific objectives formulated, relevant and cost-effective training methods and media can be selected and tailored to the learning styles of our staff. At this stage, some broad suggestions might be as follows.

(i) **On-the-job instruction and coaching** can be offered in the product/technical knowledge area by more senior staff, and those with knowledge or expertise in particular new products or processes.

(ii) **Off-the-job courses may be advisable** in the areas of customer service skills in order to give staff a new perspective and to avoid distractions. These courses could be held in-house and given by myself or the head office customer services manager: this would enable us to tailor the course to the needs identified by customer feedback, and the specific product ranges and culture of JIK. Selected individuals could be sent on external courses, and could then act as supervisors, coaches and mentors to other staff.

(iii) **Video-based training packages** on customer service are also available, and these might be a cost-effective general orientation, but more interactive methods (include role plays) will be needed to encourage the application of learning.

(iv) In the area of technical and product knowledge, we could use **resources provided by the manufacturers**: Nikon, Pentax and the others supply detailed brochures and instructional videos, and may be willing to offer the services of their own experts to brief staff, since it will enable them to on-sell their products better.

IV EVALUATING TRAINING METHODS

It is recognised that JIK would wish to monitor the direct and indirect costs of training and to ensure that anticipated benefits actually accrue. Training can be evaluated by the following means.

(i) **Monitor and appraise the work performance of the trainee** for general improvement and/or the achievement of specific training objectives.

BPP PUBLISHING

(ii)   **Monitor and appraise the work performance of the store** for the achievement of its training objectives, ensuring that any individual improvements are integrated into the work of the whole team. A follow-up customer survey may be a good way of measuring post-training improvements in customer satisfaction, and customer perceptions of improvement.

(iii) **Test post-training skills**, knowledge and competence for comparison with pre-training testing.

(iv)   Monitor and appraise the **satisfaction of trainees,** through attitude surveys and training feedback forms.

(v)   Monitor and appraise the on-going development of trainees: the impact of training on promotion/succession (creating promotable individuals), recruitment (making more skills available within the store) and so on.

(vi)   **Analyse potential indicators** of the knock-on effects of training: lower staff turnover, fewer disciplinary complaints, improved employee morale and so on.

V   EMPLOYEE DEVELOPMENT

'Development' involves more than education and training to fill knowledge and skill gaps. Employee development includes:

(i)   The development of job-relevant knowledge, skills and competence (through education and training)

(ii)   Career development: the planned progression of competent individuals through the organisation, both 'upwards' through promotion and management succession, and 'laterally' through the acquisition of wide-ranging experience;

(iii) Personal development: taking account of people's wider needs and aspirations.

Career development is valuable for the organisation because it enables a smooth flow of trusted and culture-fitted individuals into supervisory and managerial vacancies and strengthens the highly cost-effective internal labour market. It requires attention to:

(i)   The types of experience employees can acquire. It might be helpful if our supervisors rotated between sections, for example, to get to know the customers of repairs and servicing, sales, processing and so on;

(ii)   The individual's guides and role models in the organisation. On-the-job training can encourage mentoring, for example;

(iii) The level of opportunities and challenges offered to 'stretch' individuals' abilities. We could rotate supervisory duties, for example.

Even encouraging personal development can be valuable for the organisation. If our employees hone their own skills and win photographic awards, for example, it would be a wonderful advertisement for JIK's expertise.

30   INDUCTION

> **Tutor's hint**. This is an interesting question, because it invites you to consider whether there may be *disadvantages* to induction training! Note that the question addresses *formal* induction training, not an informal 'showing recruits around' session: bear this in mind when suggesting your course outline.

(a) **Advantages and disadvantages of formal induction**

The purpose of induction training is to integrate new recruits as quickly and effectively as possible into the social structure, work methods and culture of the organisation, in order to support and enable them in beginning to perform their task functions.

Advantages of formal induction training

(i)   It helps **recruits to find their bearings**, minimising the disorientation and stress of starting in an unfamiliar setting. This benefits the organisation by facilitating early performance and reducing the risk of early staff turnover.

(ii)   It **equips new recruits with the information** they require to begin performing (or learning to perform) usefully as quickly as possible.

(iii)   It **connects new recruits with the social and communication networks** that will enable co-ordinated work performance and on-going support.

(iv)   It gives **new recruits an initial positive experience** of the organisation which may contribute to morale and commitment.

(v)   It begins to **integrate recruits into the culture**, behavioural norms and values of the organisation, so that they become well adapted and committed members.

(vi)   It begins an **on-going process of training** needs identification and development planning.

The **disadvantages** of such a programme, in itself, make a less compelling argument. Induction training delays the start of on-the-job performance and may therefore frustrate recruits who are eager to 'get stuck in', while incurring unnecessary costs. However, this is short-term thinking, ignoring well-researched benefits. It may be argued with more justice that *poorly conceived or conducted* induction training may have disadvantages in creating a negative impression of the organisation, wasting time and money, teaching recruits bad habits or simply being irrelevant to recruits' needs.

(b) **Format for a formal induction course**

Step 1 A **general welcome** and briefing on the geography, structure and culture of the organisation.

Step 2 An **introductory tour** of the work facility, both for an overview of the work process and to orient the recruit to relevant amenities.

Step 3 **Briefing by the personnel manager** on HR policies and procedures: conditions of employment, access to benefits, training opportunities and so on. Guidance may be given in completing initial employment paperwork.

Step 4 **Introduction to co-workers** and other key figures (mangers, health and safety officers, union representatives and so on): ideally, appointing a co-worker (by agreement) as coach or mentor to integrate and develop the recruit on an on-going basis.

Step 5 **Briefing on relevant company policies**: discipline and grievance procedures, health and safety rules and officers, equal opportunity rights and obligations and so on.

Step 6 **Meeting with HR and/or department managers** or mentors to plan, agree and implement initial coaching and training required to commence performance.

Step 7 Involve recruits in **participative exercises** and interactions with other staff, both on the job ('sitting with Nellie') and informally (social interaction).

Step 8 **Monitor recruits' initial progress** and commence an on-going cycle of feedback, review, problem-solving and development planning.

31   THE LEARNING PROCESS

> **Tutor's hint.**   Since part (a) mentions 'approaches to learning' (not individual learning styles or methods), we have chosen to discuss the two main branches of learning psychology: the behaviourist and cognitive schools. You could, justifiably, pick other 'schools of thought' to discuss: for example, theoretical and experiential learning. Part (b) likewise lends itself to general discussion of learner motivation, objectives and feedback. Part (c) explicitly asks for Honey and Mumford's learning styles: just make sure you attach the right description to the named styles!

(a)   **Two schools of thought on learning**

(i)   The **behaviourist** or 'stimulus-response' school suggests that learning is the formation of new connections between a given stimulus (sensory input from the environment) and response (behavioural reactions or changes), based on repeated experience. We get feedback on the results of a response, which may be successful and rewarding ('positively reinforcing' the response, making us more likely to try it again next time) or unsuccessful or unpleasant ('negatively reinforcing' the response, making us more likely to avoid or change it next time).

(ii)   The **cognitive school** suggests that learning is a process whereby the human mind gathers, organises and interprets feedback information on the results of behaviours, to make rational decisions about whether to maintain or modify those behaviours, with a view to attaining goals. It is not just a stimulus, but how we think about that stimulus – what it means to us – that governs our response.

(b)   **Requirements of effective training programmes**

(i)   The individual needs to be **motivated** to learn by positive goals and/or reinforcements.

(ii)   **Clear objectives and standards** should be set, so that individuals can make meaningful decisions about the amount and direction of effort they put into the process.

(iii)   **Timely, relevant feedback** on progress should be given, to allow individuals to making learning decisions.

(iv)   **Positive and negative reinforcement** can be judiciously used to encourage or discourage learned behaviours. (Punishment usually does not work as well as recognition and encouragement.)

(v)   **Active participation** is more telling than passive reception, because it allows the establishment of stimulus-response patterns, trial-and-error reinforcement and better concentration.

(c)   **Honey and Mumford's learning styles**

Honey and Mumford put forward four predominant learning styles which suit different individuals.

(i)   **Theorists** need to understand underlying concepts prior to any hands-on attempt: their preferred approach is intellectual and rational. They prefer training programmes which are structured and theory-based, and which allow time for analysis.

(ii)   **Reflectors** need to observe or research things and think deeply about them before acting or coming to thought-out conclusions. They prefer training programmes which allow them to work at their own pace (typically, slow) and with plenty of information.

(iii)   **Activists** love to 'get stuck in': they need to work on practical tasks or problems. They prefer training based on hands-on experience and thrive on participation and challenges.

(iv)   **Pragmatists** need to see a direct link between the subject being studied and a real task or problem for which they may be responsible. Their preferred training outcome is to be able to implement an action plan or do a job better, and they thrive in on-the-job training.

32   PURPOSES AND OBJECTIVES OF APPRAISAL

> **Tutor's hint.** The point of the comment in part (a) is the belief that the only purpose for which appraisal can be used is setting pay levels. Don't be distracted by the reference to job evaluation: simply outline the full variety of purposes and objectives for appraisal. The point of the comment in part (b) is the belief that on-going informal feedback on performance by managers to subordinates is sufficient to achieve the purposes of appraisal: you should focus on the drawbacks of such an approach which formal appraisal is designed to overcome.

(a)   **The purposes of appraisal systems**

Job-evaluated pay structures award pay for factors in the job: they do not address the performance of individual job holders. Even in the case of pay awards, therefore, there is an argument for introducing an appraisal system, to help the organisation offer appropriate rewards and incentives for individual contributions over and above 'job requirements'.

However, the purposes of performance appraisal are much wider than reward review.

(i)   Establishing the key or main **results** which the individual will be expected to achieve in the course of his or her work over a period of time.

(ii)   Comparing the individual's level of **performance** against relevant standards, in order to highlight training and development needs and opportunities.

(iii)   Identifying **areas** in which work methods, technologies and other factors could be improved **to support performance**.

(iv)   Identifying potential candidates for **promotion**, for management succession planning.

(v)   Establishing an inventory of **organisational competencies** and performance levels, as a basis for human resource planning.

(vi)   Encouraging **communication about work tasks** (especially upwards) for problem-solving, co-ordination and employee involvement.

(vii)   Creating a **culture of openness** to constructive feedback, problem-solving and continuous improvement which supports flexibility and innovation.

(b)   **Why have a formal system?**

Informal feedback, as part of on-going people management, is an important part of performance management. However, there are certain benefits to formal appraisal which informal feedback does not offer.

(i)   Supervisors and managers may obtain **random impressions** of subordinates' performance, focusing on 'critical incidents' or notable successes and failures. Formal appraisal is designed to form a coherent, complete and objective picture of each individual and the complete unit.

(ii) Managers may find it easier and more pressing to recall and deal **with negative aspects of subordinates' performance**. Formal appraisal is designed to give balanced consideration to positive reinforcement and development, which is the long-term aim of human resource management.

(iii) **Informal feedback is open to bias and abuse**, since it may be given without systematic appraisal and may be received according to subjective and unchecked perceptions of what has been said. Formal appraisal requires both parties to be accountable for judgements, responses and outcomes.

(iv) **Different managers may be applying different criteria**, as well as varying standards of objectivity and judgement. Formal appraisal systems are designed to standardise relevant performance criteria.

(v) **Managers rarely, in practice, give subordinates adequate feedback** on their performance. Formal appraisal stimulates feedback and problem-solving discussion.

33   TRENDS IN APPRAISAL

> **Tutor's hint.** If three 'new approaches to appraisal' do not immediately leap to mind, work through the criticisms cited in the introduction to the question. Performance management, for example, answers the 'backward-looking' and 'perfunctory' points. Various sources and directions of feedback (including upwards) remove the 'top down' power aspects. Results-oriented approaches (as opposed to 'personality assessments') address the relevance issues. Ensure that you include 5 marks' worth of content for each approach.

New approaches to appraisal

(a) **Performance management** (PM) is a new approach to appraisal, which includes continuous collaborative planning and control. Individuals and teams jointly set key accountabilities, objectives, measures and priorities for performance and performance improvement, and review and adjust performance on an on-going basis.

This approach answers the criticisms of appraisal

(i) **PM is not primarily retrospective ('backward looking')**. Performance management focuses on the following review period, and on progress towards continuous improvement goals: it is therefore more forward-looking, pro-active and stimulating in its orientation;

(ii) **PM is not 'perfunctory'** in the sense of merely being a once-a-year, bureaucratic requirement. Performance management is an on-going control system with in-built feedback and review timescales;

(iii) **PM is not** irrelevant to job performance, because primarily focused on the (personal) development and reward aspirations of the employee. Performance management is focused on adding value to the business through the integration of employee improvement and reward goals with the strategic objectives of the business.

(b) **Multi-source feedback** is a new approach which gathers appraisal information from different sources:

(i) The **appraisees** themselves. Self-appraisal helps individuals to see their goals in the light of organisation and unit objectives, and removes the element of judgement from appraisal.

(ii)   The **appraisees' subordinates**. Upward appraisal offers meaningful feedback on leadership skills, empowers staff and encourages upward communication.

(iii)   **Customers (internal or external)**. Customer feedback likewise offers meaningful appraisal of customer service skills, and improves customer relations and loyalty.

(iv)   **Multiple sources**. 360-degree appraisal gathers feedback from a range of stakeholders in an individual's performance: suppliers, customers, peers, subordinates and superiors.

This approach minimises the perception of appraisal as superiors passing judgement on subordinates –an application of 'top down' political or personal control. It is also more relevant to the job, since aspects of performance (such as leadership and customer care) are assessed by those directly affected by them.

(c)   **Results-oriented criteria** reflect a new approach to appraisal, in which performance is measured against specific targets and standards of performance. This is a change from personality based appraisal systems which took as their criteria for assessment a range of personal qualities (loosely defined as 'personality traits') such as intelligence, reliability, initiative and so on. Job- or results-oriented systems take as their criteria factors defined as being important for successful job performance: depending on the approach used these may be based on critical incidents, key results or competencies, as derived from job analysis, job descriptions, competency definitions or the plans, targets and standards set for the individual or unit.

Results-oriented approaches answer the criticism that appraisal is irrelevant to job performance, since the criteria for assessment are directly related to job performance and improvement.

34   EVALUATING APPRAISAL

> **Tutor's hint.** This is an unstructured question, which may pose time and information management issues. Decide in advance how many main points you wish to discuss and work out your own mark allocation from there. (We have chosen six factors to be monitored, allowing under three marks for each.) Sort out in your own mind what the question is asking. What *factors* or *outcomes* should be *monitored* in order to evaluate the success of appraisal schemes? (In other words, what methods of evaluation will be used?) And what *criteria* will be measured by each of these methods? (In other words, how is 'successful appraisal' defined in terms of specific performance indicators.)

Appraising appraisal systems

Factors/outcomes to be monitored	Evaluating what criteria?
The perceptions, attitudes and feelings of appraisers and appraisees about the process (as expressed in attitude surveys, feedback forms or interviews)	Is the appraisal system taken seriously? Is the system perceived to be fair and useful? Are appraisers able to be honest/constructive? Do appraisees feel threatened/judged or supported and involved in performance improvement?

Factors/outcomes to be monitored	Evaluating what criteria?
Individual and unit performance results (across a range of specific performance criteria and standards)	Has appraisal resulted in problem-solving and development with the effect of enhanced performance?
Training provision and outcomes	Has appraisal resulted in identification of relevant training needs? Has appraisal resulted in take-up of training and development opportunities?
Promotions and management succession plans	Has appraisal identified promotable individuals? Has appraisal resulted in training and development allowing smooth promotional transitions?
Other human resource indicators, such as staff turnover, absenteeism, disciplinary actions and so on	Has constructive appraisal resulted in employee motivation, morale and commitment to jointly-agreed goals?
Time, costs and resources spent on appraisal, compared with quantified and qualitative benefits in performance improvements and employee morale	Is the system efficiently organised? Is it cost-effective?

35 THE IMPORTANCE OF HEALTH AND SAFETY

> **Tutor's hint.** This question requires you to think about health and safety on a different level than merely statutory provisions and preventive measures. In part (a) think through the *business* arguments for health and safety (What are the benefits to the organisation of a safe, healthy workforce? What are the costs of failure in this area?), as well as the humane or ethical arguments. Part (b) is essentially asking why law and regulation is insufficient to ensure safe and healthy working.

(a) **The importance of health and safety at work**

(i)   It is **humane and ethical** to protect employees (and other visitors to the organisation) from the risk of pain and suffering.

(ii)   Employers and employees alike have **legal obligations** to provide and support a safe and healthy working environment under UK statute (which incorporates EU directives) and common law. Failure to comply can lead to warnings, enforced shut-down of unsafe systems and financial penalties – as well as prosecution by affected parties, with the threat of awards for damages.

(iii) Accidents, illness and other causes of employee absence and/or impaired performance cost the organisation **money** in lost work time and output, labour replacement costs, repairs and so on.

(iv)   The **morale and performance** of employees will suffer if they are forced to work in an environment in which they feel unsafe, insecure and un-valued by the organisation.

(v)   A poor health and safety record will affect **employee loyalty** and the organisation's employer brand in the labour market. This will impair its ability to attract and retain skilled labour, which may be particularly damaging where is competing for scarce skills.

(vi)   A poor health and safety record will affect **public relations in general,** damaging the organisation's image in the market place to which it sells good and services and from which it gets its materials and resources.

(b)   **Why do health and safety problems persist?**

(i)   **Legislation merely sets a minimal standard of protection:** 'the law is a floor'. It does not represent satisfactory – let alone best – practice for ethical and socially responsible organisations. Organisations can 'get away with' basic standards in markets where labour is plentiful and the market less demanding in terms of ethical values.

(ii)   Health and safety are regarded with a **negative attitude by many managers.** Provisions are costly and have no immediately quantifiable benefit. Charles Hampden-Turner (*Corporate Culture)* suggests that organisation cultures can actively suppress health and safety values, by:

- Emphasising 'macho-individualism' over 'safety first'

- Seeing safety as the responsibility of specialists rather than everyone's responsibility

- Seeing safety as a threat to productivity and so on

(iii)   **Positive discipline** – setting mechanisms, policies and systems which theoretically prevent hazardous behaviour – only goes so far. Irresponsible and ignorant behaviour can still cause accidents.

(iv)   **New health and safety concerns are constantly emerging.** New technology and ergonomics, for example, have made physical labour less fatiguing and stressful but have created health risks associated with sedentary lifestyle, isolation, radiation, repetitive strain injury and so on.

36   THE COST OF ACCIDENTS

> **Tutor's hint.** This is a fairly straightforward question in the health and safety area, as long as you bear in mind the full range of potential costs of accidents.

(a)   **Potential costs to employers of accidents at work**

- Time lost by the injured employee

- Time lost by other employees who choose to (or must) stop work as a result of the accident

- Time lost by supervisors, managers, safety and maintenance staff through investigation, reporting, counselling, repair and other duties following an accident

- A proportion of the cost of maintaining first aid materials and trained staff

- Lost output as a result of disruption to operations

- Cost of replacement, repair or modification of equipment as a result of accidental damage or unsafe use

- Costs associated with increased insurance premiums following claims

- Reduced output from the injured employee on return to work

- Reduced output as a result of poor employee morale, increased absenteeism, increased labour turnover among employees and so on, if they feel their work is unsafe and they are not being protected

- Costs of recruiting, training or redeploying replacements for injured workers

(b) **Steps to reduce the frequency and severity of accidents**

Step 1 Formulating a comprehensive, rigorous and relevant safety policy.

Step 2 Developing safety consciousness as part of the organisation culture: emphasising that safety is everyone's responsibility (not only that of safety officers or specialists) and that safety is a key value and priority of the business.

Step 3 Developing effective consultative participation between management, workers and trade unions so that safety rules are accepted and supported.

Step 4 Giving adequate instruction and training in safety rules and measures, especially for new or transferred workers and where methods have been changed.

Step 5 Minimising and managing known hazards such as materials handling, moving parts, hazardous substances and so on.

Step 6 Enforcing stringent maintenance standards for plant and fittings (such as safety guards and shut-offs).

Step 7 Monitoring general maintenance of the work environment to ensure that hazards (such as worn or slippery flooring) are controlled.

37 STRESS

> **Tutor's hint.** This is a straightforward question in terms of content, but it offers a useful lesson in topic key words. You could hardly miss that the question is about stress – but check that you have correctly identified 'symptoms' (how stress manifests itself in people), 'causes' or 'aggravators' (things that make people stressed, or make their stress worse) and 'techniques for managing' (not avoiding) stress.

(a) **Symptoms of stress**

(i)   **Nervous tension** may manifest itself in various ways: irritability, increased sensitivity, preoccupation with details, black and white perceptions of issues, sleeplessness – and various physical symptoms such as skin and digestive disorders, tension headaches and so on.

(ii) **Withdrawal** is a defence mechanism which may manifest itself in unusual quietness, reluctance to communicate, or physical withdrawal in the form of absenteeism and poor time-keeping.

(iii) **Low morale** may show itself in low confidence, depressed body language, lack of interest and expressions of frustration, worthlessness or hopelessness.

(iv) Signs that the individual is **repressing the problem** and trying too hard to appear to be coping: forced cheerfulness, boisterous playfulness or excessive drinking may indicate this.

None of these symptoms on their own necessarily indicate stress, but a number of them together should alert an individual's colleagues to the possibility of stress-related causes.

(b) **Causes or aggravators of stress**

(i)   **Personality type:** competitive, sensitive and insecurely boundaried people are more prone to stress and feel it more acutely.

(ii) **Role ambiguity and conflict:** a person may experience stress if he is unsure what is expected of him in a given situation, or where conflicting demands are placed on him by different roles (eg family and work)

(iii) **Risk, change and responsibility** can cause stress – particularly in combination. Insecurity and uncertainty are often perceived as stressful, and this is aggravated by the perceived severity of the consequences of failure or error.

(iv) **Management style** was identified by US research as a cause of stress and related health problems. Particularly stress-inducing traits included unpredictability, destruction of workers' self-esteem and setting up win/lose dilemmas.

(v) **Workload** is a cause of stress: ironically, this applies to the frustration of insufficient stimulation ('underload') as well as 'overload'.

(c) **Stress management techniques**

Some stress is helpful, stimulating motivation and creativity: thus, we do not talk about 'abolishing' stress. Techniques for managing the severity and symptoms of stress include:

- **Time off,** including regular rest breaks and/or rotation of tasks, to provide variety, change of perspective and opportunities for rest and relaxation.

- **Relaxation techniques,** such as biodata feedback, breathing exercises and various forms of meditation, which are designed to deepen breathing, slow heart rate and generally moderate the body's 'flight or fight' reactions to stress.

- **Physical exercise** and creative self-expression, as a safety value for tensions and a working off of adrenalin released into the blood stream by stress.

- **Counselling,** to raise awareness of thought patterns and beliefs (such as poor boundaries, over-responsibility and so on) that may be contributing to stress.

- **Training in skills that address the work problems** which create or aggravate stress: for example, time management skills (to minimise workload-related stressors), assertiveness (to strengthen boundaries) and so on.

38 SCENARIO: THEORIES OF MOTIVATION

> **Tutor's hint.** This is a reasonably complex scenario for the purposes of answering part (d) on the specific motivational issues involved, but should otherwise offer the opportunity to demonstrate your understanding of various motivation theories. Note the variety of instruction keywords: 'distinguish' (highlight the differences between); 'explain' (clarify the meaning); 'critically evaluate' (highlight good and bad points); 'identify' (pick out); and 'outline' (list with brief explanations). In part (d), whether you discuss needs, factors or expectancy, you should note Ben's likely income requirements, apparent aspirations as a computer programmer and (from earlier in the scenario) freedom to take on freelance work elsewhere. In Ann's case, think about motivations in light of her age and possible social isolation.

(a) **Content and process theories**

(i) **Content theories** of motivation ask the questions: 'What are the things that motivate people'? They are based on the belief that human beings have an innate set of needs or desired outcomes and that behaviour is driven and determined (motivated) by the desire to satisfy those needs or achieve those outcomes.

Maslow's 'hierarchy of needs' and Herzberg's 'two factor theory' are both content theories.

(ii) *Process* theories of motivation ask the question: 'how are people motivated?' or 'how can they be motivated (by others, such as a superior at work)?' They focus on the processes through which:

- Outcomes become desirable to an individual

- Individuals select particular behaviours in order to pursue desirable outcomes

- Individuals calculate whether it is worth implementing and maintaining those behaviours in order to achieve those outcomes

Vroom's expectancy theory and Handy's motivation calculus are examples of process theories.

(b) **Theory X and Theory Y**

Douglas McGregor formulated Theory X and Theory Y to reflect two extreme sets of managerial assumptions about worker motivation: they are not 'types of people'.

(i) *Theory X* is based on the belief that the average human being dislikes work and will avoid it if possible.

- People must be coerced, controlled, directed and/or threatened with sanctions in order to get them to make an adequate effort.

- People fear responsibility and want security above all.

- A manager who operates on the basis of Theory X will feel (s)he has to direct and control workers with specific instructions, close supervision, rigid task structures and carrot-and-stick incentives.

(ii) *Theory Y* is based on the belief that the expenditure of physical and mental effort in work is as natural as play or rest: the average human being does not inherently dislike work: according to the conditions it may be a source of satisfaction or deprivation.

- People are motivated by the desire for personal growth and achievement and are capable of exercising self-direction and self-control.

- A manager who operates on the basis of Theory Y will try to integrate subordinates' needs for development and self-expression with the organisation's objectives, so that both can be achieved together. (S)he will tend to use a democratic or consultative style of management.

(c) **Maslow's hierarchy of needs**

Maslow's theory is easy to grasp and has a certain intuitive appeal: but the theory is not very useful in practice for a manager wishing to motivate a team. (To be fair, Maslow did not specifically intend his theory to be used in such a context.)

(i) It is **difficult to identify where an individual** is in the hierarchy: a given behaviour may be motivated by a number of different needs.

(ii) It is **difficult to predict behaviour** on the basis of where the individual is in the hierarchy: he may satisfy a given need in any number of ways.

(iii) It is difficult to design reward systems on the basis of the hierarchy. The place of pay and the nature of self-actualisation are particularly ambiguous.

In addition, the theory has certain internal weaknesses.

(i) It ignores phenomena such as deferred gratification and altruism, which overturn the 'hierarchy of relative pre-potency'.

(ii)   It is difficult to verify in practice – particularly in other cultural contexts.

(d) **Issues in the motivation of Anne and Ben**

Anne

(i)   In terms of **content theories**, one might expect that Anne will have high needs for:

- Social interaction and belonging, since she is widowed and living alone

- Security, since she is now 50 and may not be confident of her career mobility

- Recognition and esteem, since she has completed her child-rearing tasks and may be seeking self-worth in rebuilding a career

(ii)   In terms of **expectancy**, Anne is likely to have a strong expectation – having used her skills to good effect in a larger company – that she can achieve a good level of performance in her current job. If PQR can offer her rewards with high valence or importance to her (such as satisfaction of the needs set out above), she will be well motivated to apply her skills.

(iii)   **The question is: since one of Anne's prime needs is job security, does PQR need to incur the costs of offering any incentive over and above continuing employment?** If we wish to secure Anne's *best* efforts, however, we could apply **positive rewards** in the form of greater opportunities **for team-working and recognition.** If we can involve her in the customer care committee, for example, or in coaching the engineers in book-keeping skills, we will not only reap the benefits of Anne's greater enthusiasm for her work, but may get spin-off benefits for the business.

Ben

(i)   In terms of content theories, one might expect that Ben will have high needs for:

- Security – particularly financial, since he has new family responsibilities and will have certain financial aspirations and obligations at this 'career takeoff' stage of the family lifecycle

- Self-actualisation, since Ben appears to be seeking to develop his skills in the computing field on his own initiative

(ii)   In terms of **expectancy**, these needs create **high valency** – but there may not be any great expectation that they can be met by successful performance in Ben's current job. He appears to be seeking more profitable career avenues elsewhere, in computer programming.

(iii)   This poses a problem for PQR, especially since the engineers are on flexible contracts, facilitating Ben in developing his own business at the expense of his long-term commitment to PQR.

(iv)   We will need to consider whether we can (and are prepared) to offer Ben the incentives required to retain his skills and loyalty: more information will be required to make this decision. In the short term, bonus rates of pay or higher guaranteed hours may hold him – but in the longer term, it may be worth investigating opportunities for a computer programmer in the PQR offices or as part of our services to clients.

(e) **Management objectives of a reward system**

    (i)   It should enable the organisation to **attract and retain the people and skills required by its human resource plan.** (In other words, rewards offered should compare sufficiently favourably with market rates to attract workers of the required calibre into the organisation and to avoid causing dissatisfaction that might encourage labour turnover.)

    (ii)   It should increase the **predictability of employees' behaviour,** by reliably offering effective incentives for them to behave in desired ways, and positive reinforcement when they do so.

    (iii)   It should **increase employees' willingness to accept change and flexibility,** by applying incentives and positive reinforcement for flexible behaviour, and by offering the security and motivation required to overcome resistance to change.

    (iv)   It should **encourage innovative thinking and behaviour** (since this is a key strategy for survival and growth).

    (v)   It should **motivate employees**: that is, it should secure adequate or increased commitment and effort towards the organisation's goals.

    (vi)   It **should reflect the nature of jobs in the organisation and the skills/knowledge/experience required to perform them.** This is an important element in all of the above, because rewards depend for their effectiveness on people's perceptions of them. Pay, in particular, can cause as much de-motivation as motivation. Consistency, objective job evaluation and performance appraisal, and the preservation of differentials to reflect ability and responsibility, are essential in order for the system to be perceived as fair and therefore to offer a meaningful incentive to performance.

39   THE JOB AS A MOTIVATOR

> **Tutor's hint.** The reference to Herzberg should have alerted you to the source of the theory on which the question is based. This would have helped if you did not know that 'environmental' factors are another name for 'hygiene' factors, and should have suggested areas for discussion in part (b): Herzberg's theories of job rotation, job enlargement and job enrichment. (We have chosen to evaluate two of these, alongside the micro-design of jobs, for contrast.) Remember to evaluate each of the three methods: not to compare them with each other.

(a) **Environmental and motivator factors**

Environmental or hygiene factors, in Herzberg's model, are those which satisfy the need to avoid unpleasantness: they may (temporarily) prevent job dissatisfaction, but they will not by themselves produce motivation or positive and lasting job satisfaction. They are basically factors related to conditions at work: examples include salary, supervisory style and working conditions.

Motivator factors are those which satisfy the need for personal growth: they are able to motivate and provide positive, lasting job satisfaction. They are basically factors integral to the job itself: examples include challenging work, variety, responsibility and a sense of achievement.

(b) **Job design for intrinsic rewards**

'Intrinsic' rewards are those which integral to the job and within the perception of the worker: sense of achievement, interest, responsibility and so on. Job design may offer more or less of these kinds of rewards.

(i)   The **micro-design** of jobs became popular in manufacturing industries after the Scientific Management school pioneered by FW Taylor put forward ideas such as task specialisation and efficiency of motions.

In terms of intrinsic rewards, the micro-design of jobs is lacking in all five factors identified as key dimensions of job satisfaction:

- Skill variety (since workers are trained to fulfil single repetitive motions)

- Task identity and significance (since they are 'small cogs' in a big machine)

- Autonomy (since they are expected to perform in accordance with the 'science' of work imposed by management)

- Feedback (since the work and its 'science' are separated: workers are not expected to understand their role)

(ii)   **Job enlargement** was put forward by Herzberg as one method of job re-design which would enhance the intrinsic rewards of work.

Job enlargement is a 'horizontal' extension of the individual's work by increasing the number of operations or tasks in which he is involved. This has the effect of reducing repetition and increasing task and skill variety.

Job enlargement is limited in its intrinsic rewards, since asking a worker to complete three separate tedious, unchallenging tasks is unlikely to motivate him more than asking to fulfil just one tedious, unchallenging task!

(iii) **Job enrichment** was put forward by Herzberg as the most effective method of job re-design for enhancing the intrinsic rewards of work.

Job enrichment is planned, deliberate action to build greater responsibility, breadth and challenge into a job. It is thus a 'vertical' extension of the job design by:

- Removing controls (increasing autonomy)
- Providing direct performance information (increasing feedback)
- Introducing new tasks and special assignments (increasing skill variety)
- Adding accountability (increasing task identity and significance)

Job enrichment (which may be equated with modern approaches to 'empowerment') offers significant rewards in each of the key dimensions of job satisfaction. However, intrinsic rewards should not be regarded as a substitute for extrinsic rewards. Handy notes that 'even those who want their jobs enriched will expect to be rewarded with more than job satisfaction.'

40   PAY AS A MOTIVATOR

Tutor's hint. The reference to Frederick Herzberg in the introduction should have suggested some of the points to be included in part (a): pay is *only* a hygiene factor (and therefore its effectiveness as a motivator is limited) but it is the most *important* of the hygiene factors, and can represent a way of attaining motivator factors such as status and recognition (so it will be a key component of any reward strategy). Remember that the instruction keyword 'evaluate' means considering benefits and drawbacks/limitations: present a balanced argument. In part (b), it is the topic keywords that are important: ensure that you describe methods of *determining* the level and structure of pay – not different types of monetary reward.

(a)   **Effectiveness of pay as a motivator**

Financial incentives occupy a central, but ambiguous, role in motivation theories. On the one hand, pay can be seen as effective motivators.

(i) In Maslow's need theory, **money** does not feature explicitly, but it is likely to be **instrumental in satisfying other needs**: buying food and shelter, representing status and worth and so on.

(ii) Herzberg likewise recognised that pay could **be converted into a wide range of other satisfactions** and represented a consistent measure of the worth or value of the individual.

(iii) Schein's 'Economic Man' model suggests that people will adjust their effort if offered money to do so.

People need money to live, so it will certainly be part of the reward 'package' an individual demands from work. However, it is not the sole motivator, nor an effective motivator for all individuals in all circumstances.

(i) Monetary rewards cannot by themselves satisfy what Maslow identified as **'higher order'** needs for love, esteem and self-actualisation.

(ii) Herzberg identified pay as a 'hygiene' factor, not a **'motivator'**: it must be managed to minimise dissatisfaction, but is not a source of lasting satisfaction or incentive to enhanced performance.

(iii) There are particular problems with monetary incentives. They can **encourage purely 'instrumental' performance**, conflicting with quality, safety, team-working and so on.

(b) **Methods of setting pay levels and structures**

Other than legal requirements (such as the minimum wage in the UK), there are four main factors in determining pay.

(i) **Job evaluation**: a systematic process of analysing job components (not the merit of the job-holder) in order to establish the relative worth or 'value' of jobs within an organisation, so that differentials, grades and levels of pay can be developed in a fair and equitable manner (which is acceptable under Equal Pay legislation).

(ii) **Negotiation and collective agreements on pay**. Scales, differentials and minimum rates may have been negotiated between management and employee representatives (eg trade unions or staff associations) at plant, local or national level.

(iii) **Market rates**. Market rates of pay will have most influence on pay structures where there is a standard pattern of supply and demand in the open labour market. If an organisation's rates fall below the benchmark rates in the market from which it recruits, it will have trouble attracting and retaining skilled employees.

(iv) **Individual performance in the job**. Pay scales should allow for merit awards for above-standard performance (as defined and measured by the organisation's appraisal system). In addition, there may be individual, team or factory-wide performance-related pay components (bonuses, profit-sharing and so on).

41 MANAGERS AND LEADERS

> **Tutor's hint.** This should be familiar territory. Its major challenge may be answering part (a) without having to duplicate your remarks in part (b) or (c): each part should, in fact, give you helpful ideas for the next. Note the different instruction key words: 'describe' (say what it consists of); 'distinguish' (highlight the differences between); and 'explain' (give reasons for). This is a useful discipline in reading and selecting questions and planning answers.

(a) **What is leadership?**

Leadership is the process of influencing others to work willingly towards goals.

   (i) Leadership is an **interpersonal process**: it depends on relationships, communication and influence – not organisational authority.

   (ii) **'The essence of leadership is followership.'** (Koontz, O'Donnell, Weihrich) The leader's power depends on the perceptions of others: it is conferred from below, not delegated from above.

   (iii) Leadership is the 'influential increment over and above mechanical compliance with the routine directives of the organisation' (Katz and Kahn). **Compliance – or obedience – may be sufficient for routine work, but the modern flexible organisation increasingly requires extra input from employees: cooperation, effort, creativity, acceptance of change and so on.**

(b) **Management and leadership activities**

Management can be exercised over resources, activities, projects and other essentially non-personal things. Management involves activities concerned with structure, analysis and control, aimed at producing predictable outputs from planned inputs: for example, planning and budgeting, organisation and staffing, controlling and problem-solving.

Leadership can only be exercised over people. Leadership, on the other hand, requires a completely different set of activities aimed at influencing, persuading, enthusing and guiding people.

   (i) Creating a sense of direction (often, something different to the status quo)

   (ii) Communicating a vision (particular powerful if it meets the needs of others, or if the leader gives it credibility)

   (iii) Energising, inspiring and motivating others to translate the vision into achievement

   (iv) Creating the culture that will support the achievement.

(c) **Why is leadership important?**

Leadership skills have become important because of the level and type of performance they are able to draw from people. Organisations, particularly those operating in business environments requiring flexibility, responsiveness and innovation, require the following

   (i) **Commitment.** Leadership, by communicating vision, secures commitment: management secures obedience – which by definition is incapable of going beyond the rules.

   (ii) **Creativity and flexibility.** Leadership directs employees' energies towards the organisation's mission and objectives, facilitating 'outside the box' thinking

   (iii) **Self-responsibility.** Leadership facilitates empowerment, which allows efficient and flexible use of the human resource.

(iv) Highly skilled and flexible workers have come to expect empowerment: leadership skills are required to attract and retain such workers in competition with other employers.

(v) There are fewer job descriptions and procedures to rely on in competency-based, project-management organisations: control based on interpersonal skills is likely to adapt better to such an environment than a framework of formal authority and defined roles.

42   LEADERSHIP STYLE

> **Tutor's hint.**   This is an unstructured question, which means that you will need to impose your own structure on it. The instruction key words 'critically discuss' suggest an approach: you need to present arguments for and against the assertions and assumptions made by the quoted statement. First, analyse what assertions and assumptions it is making. We suggest there are actually three: (a) that managers can choose leadership styles; (b) that a leadership style can ever be 'entirely appropriate' to a given situation and that (c) this is an important skill for managers. This gives a coherent structure (and target mark allocation) for our answer.

(a) **A leadership style can be chosen to fit the situation**

Early theorists concentrated on the 'traits' that successful leaders were said to 'possess'. However, the 'great man' theory failed to describe or facilitate the dynamics of the leadership situation.

It came to be recognised that a 'style' of leadership – a strategic pattern of attitudes and behaviours – could be adopted, and that different styles appeared to be effective in different contexts, according to such variables as the relationship between the leader and the group, the nature of the task and the power of the leader in relation to the group (Fiedler).

It therefore seemed desirable for a would-be leader to select and adopt a style for 'best fit' (Handy) with the situation, as suggested in the quote.

(i) Not all would-be leaders will have the behavioural flexibility to change style convincingly to suit the situation, or to adopt a style which is not 'natural' to them

(ii) Consistency is important to subordinates, and they may regard a constantly changing 'contingency' approach to leadership style with insecurity or mistrust.

(b) **It is possible to choose a leadership style which is 'entirely appropriate' to any given situation**

Various **contingency theories** of leadership suggest a complex mix of **variables** in the leadership context, including (in John Adair's model) the **task needs, group needs** and **individual needs** of the group members and leader, as well as the 'total situation' which dictates the relative priority to be given to each set of needs.

At best, effective leadership consists of creating a balance **or 'best fit' between the different (and often conflicting) demands of all these factors**. Arguably, no style can be considered 'entirely appropriate' to all factors in a situation: from whose perspective is the 'appropriateness' to be judged?

It is important to be realistic in one's expectations of managers and of theoretical tools such as the concept of leadership style.

(c) **Choosing an appropriate style is one of the most important skills of an effective manager**

Style theorists agree that choosing an appropriate style is the key to effective management. Fiedler, for example, concluded that 'group performance will be contingent upon the appropriate matching of leadership styles and the degree of favourableness of the group situation for the leader.'

43   TEAMS AND LEADERS

> **Tutor's hint.** Contingency approaches may seem vague ('it all depends') but they have great credibility in the current organisational climate of change and flexibility. Don't neglect models such as Adair's 'action-centred' or 'situational' leadership. The discussion of Handy allows you to connect the syllabus topics of team working and leadership. Note the mark allocation of the question parts, and resist the temptation to write 10 marks' worth of content on part (b) because its topic is more familiar: you'll still only get 5 marks maximum!

(a)   **Action-centred leadership**

The action-centred (also called the 'situational' and 'functional') model of leadership was developed by John Adair. Like other contingency thinkers, Adair argued that the common perception of leadership was inadequate to describe the range of action required by the complex situation in which managers find themselves.

He described a **context** made up of three main interrelated variables: **task needs, group needs and individual needs. The overall leadership situation dictates the relative priority that must be given to each of the three sets of needs.** Effective leadership is identifying and acting on those priorities to create a balance between the needs.

The meeting of the various needs can be expressed as specific management roles.

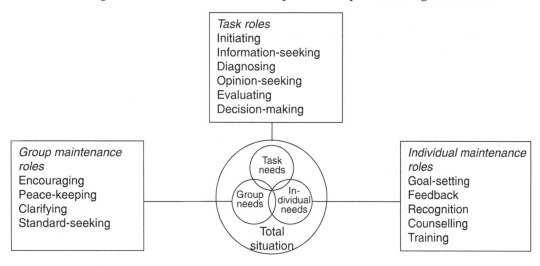

(Adair)

Around this framework, Adair developed a scheme of leadership training based on precept and practice in each of eight leadership activities – as applied to the task, team and individual: defining the task, planning, briefing, controlling, evaluating, motivating, organising and setting an example.

(b)   **The role of the leader in team effectiveness**

Charles Handy's contingency model suggests that team effectiveness depends on a number of related variables.

The givens: The team (roles, relationships and dynamics)
                       The task (nature, structure and technology of the work)
                       The environment (physical surroundings, inter-group relations)

Intervening factors: Motivation of the team
Leadership style
Processes and procedures

Outcomes: Productivity of the team
Satisfaction of team members

The leader thus occupies a central role in 'converting' the givens into positive outcomes, through his own style of operating and ability to motivate the team. At the same time, the ability of a manager to lead the team effectively will be influenced by the context: the power held by the leader in the organisation and within the team, the 'raw material' provided by the givens and so on. Handy argues that the most effective style of leadership in any particular situation is one that brings leader, subordinates and task into a 'best fit' for the situation.

44 SCENARIO: IMPROVING COMMUNICATION IN ORGANISATIONS

> **Tutor's hint.** Even from the information given, you should be able to diagnose some of the communication problems in the TUV scenario. Independent teams require efficient lines of communication: in this case, messages are failing to come across quickly and clearly. You may have identified the potential for cultural/language/perception barriers between the engineers, sales staff and work planners. You were also pointed by part (d) of the question to problems in upward communication: the fact that team feedback and suggestions were not being heard. Given this background, the content of the question should be fairly straightforward – as long as you answer the specific questions set. An effective technique is to add a header to each section of your answer (as we do) which defines what you take the question to be about: use it to cross-check that your answer is relevant and on-target.

(a) **Importance of good communication**

'Good communication' may be defined as communication which is efficient and effective in achieving its purpose.

Good communication is vitally important, particularly in a business organisation such as TUV, because the achievement of organisational objectives depends on these factors

- Exchange of information for planning, decision-making and control between different units (such as head office and maintenance teams)

- Giving of orders and instructions for operations (including job specifications for maintenance teams)

- Establishing and maintenance of working relationships, (so that, for example, on-site teams feel they are a valued part of the organisation) for co-ordination and employee morale

- Exchange of information for problem-solving and improved customer care (such as teams' feedback on co-ordination problems)

- Communication of a positive image of the organisation and its services to customers and potential customers.

If communication is ineffective, none of the above will be achieved: instructions may not be carried out on time, or errors may be made; management may not be made aware of problems; customers may be given a poor impression of the service and reliability of the organisation; lack of opportunities to communicate upwards may lower the morale of employees; co-ordination will suffer, and inter-unit conflict may result. We are seeing all the above symptoms of poor communication in TUV.

If communication is inefficient, there will be a waste of resources (including staff time clarifying and correcting misunderstandings) and poor control and co-ordination, for which the organisation is accountable to its stakeholders.

(b) **Ten major barriers to good communication**

(i) **Poor basic communication skills** on the part of senders (giving distorted messages, for example) or receivers (inattentive listening, for example).

(ii) **Failure to give or seek feedback.** Feedback – the response which confirms or questions accurate receipt of a message – is essential to effective communication.

(iii) **Misinterpretation or ignorance of non-verbal communication.** Non-verbal messages may confirm or contradict verbal ones, and are often a source of misinterpretation.

(iv) **Differences in language.** Sales people, planning specialists and road engineers may not relate to each other's technical jargon or symbols.

(v) **Personal differences, or 'social noise'.** Differences in age, gender, education, ethnic origin and task culture will encourage different perceptions and interpretations of messages, with potential for misunderstanding.

(vi) **Conflict**, which may create unwillingness to communicate helpfully. Withholding or distorting information may reflect lack of respect, hostility or political game-playing.

(vii) **Inappropriate amount or accuracy of information.** Information may be either excessive or insufficient for its purpose.

(viii) **Active or implied discouragement of communication.** An organisation may, for example, ignore or respond negatively to input or the exchange of information. (The maintenance crews feel this is happening at TUV.)

(ix) Lack of trust in the source. If the source of the message is unknown, or regarded without respect, it may be rejected.

(x) **Poor communication channels, media and technology.** Staff who are physically separated from the organisational centre, especially if they are on the move, need to be linked to it by efficient and effective communication systems and tools (mobile phones, regular contact routines and so on).

(c) **Overcoming communication barriers**

In broad terms, the barriers to good communication can be overcome by addressing their underlying causes. A flexible contingency approach will be the key, because there is no universal formula for every situation – especially in organisations which by their nature draw together diverse functions, personalities and priorities. (It will be particularly important to seek input and feedback from TUV staff in all units prior to formulating communication policy, since failure to do this is one of the major problems.)

(i) **Communication can be encouraged, facilitated and rewarded.** Status and functional barriers (particularly to upward communication and communication between engineers and head office staff) can be minimised by improving opportunities (such as the planning committee) for formal and informal networking and feedback.

(ii) **Training and guidance** can be given in communication skills, including consideration of audience needs, listening, giving feedback and so on.

(iii) **People can be made aware of the potential for misunderstanding** arising from differences in perception and work culture, and taught to consider others' viewpoints.

(iv) **Technology, systems and procedures can be adapted** to facilitate communication: making it more effective (clearer mobile phone reception), faster (laptops for the e-mailing of instructions) and more consistent (regular reporting routines).

(v) **Conflict and organisational politics** can be managed so that no basic unwillingness to communicate exists between units. Measures may range from specific conflict resolution to adjusting TUV's culture to appreciate diversity and focus on customer service.

(d) **Problems of upward communication and how they can be overcome**

(i) Teams think that management will not be interested in or able to understand their problems, opinions or information input.

(ii) Teams think that management are too busy, or are being given too much other information, to give their attention to such matters.

(iii) Teams fear the consequences of communicating: 'shooting the messenger', being rejected, stepping out from the work group.

(iv) There is genuinely no apparatus or opportunity for upward communication beyond the formal minimum (grievance procedures, reporting requirements, trade union negotiations).

The problem at TUV is primarily the first of these, since a formal channel for upward communication does exist (in the form of the planning meeting) but is not allowing teams to feel heard or taken seriously.

The organisation needs a **system which offers a channel for employees' complaints**, comments and suggestions as to how work practices, systems or technology might be improved or problems solved. This may be achieved by a number of means.

(i) More regular non-negotiatory meetings with employee representatives.

(ii) More frequent inter-unit meetings for 'brainstorming' solutions to problems or discussing work issues (in addition to the formal 'planning committee' which reviews upcoming schedules).

(iii) Quality or service 'circles' in which selected employees from all levels and functions get together to discuss quality and service-related issues.

(iv) 'Suggestion schemes', perhaps with incentives for positive contributions.

(v) 'Open door': team co-ordinators should be available to discuss problems, suggestions or feedback with team members (especially 'touching base' with maintenance team members when they are at head office).

Ultimately, however, the organisation will need to address the cultural issues (team members' disillusionment with head office, head office's apparent lack of respect for team input). This can only be done by senior management example, re-education, and reinforcement through development and reward programmes.

(e) **Brief guidelines on using the planning committee more effectively**

(i) Appoint a **committee leader** who will model effective communication and guide discussion so that all views are heard and respected.

(iii) **Re-appraise the membership of the committee**: ensure that representatives from each unit have sufficient status and influence to contribute meaningfully to the work of the committee and to command the respect of other members.

(iii) **Ensure that the committee has well-defined** terms of reference: allocate authority and responsibility for outcomes, to ensure that input is properly considered and acted upon where appropriate.

(iv) **Ensure that minutes are taken and circulated**, so that views expressed cannot be 'swept under the carpet' and so that action responsibilities are clearly allocated in writing.

(v) **Encourage informal networking and relationship-building** among committee members (perhaps including inter-unit transfers of committee members) to foster better understanding and appreciation of each other's work cultures and priorities.

45   COMMUNICATION MEDIA AND METHODS

> **Tutor's hint.** We have taken 'methods' of communication to refer to the broad forms of communication (written, oral and so on) as opposed to 'media' (such as a telephone call or letter) or 'channels' (such as the postal system or internet). If you used another interpretation, make sure you state clearly what it is – and don't forget to give the media examples. Do also remember that 'media' is the plural of 'medium'!

(a) **Five main communication methods**

(i) **Written verbal communication**: messages written and/or displayed in words, via media such as memos, letters, notices and reports. Electronic media such as the e-mail, web pages, fax and document scanning are also 'written' communication, although they can also be highly 'visual'.

(ii) **Written non-verbal (visual) communication**: messages visually depicted and/or displayed but without words, including media such as photographs, slides and videos, and written media (memos, letters, reports and so on) including diagrams and numerical or statistical data.

(iii) **Oral verbal communication**: spoken messages in words. This may occur where the parties are present or 'face to face', in a meeting or interview, or remote from each other, via media such as the telephone, video-conferencing or web-cast.

(iv) **Oral non-verbal communication**: 'spoken' messages not involving words, including sounds (such as sighs, silence, throat clearing or inarticulate expressions like 'huh?') which are often used in giving feedback.

(v) **Other non-verbal communication**: messages conveyed by, for example, body language, facial expression, gestures, position, appearance and so on.

(b) **Factors influencing the choice of communication medium**

(i) The **time necessary** (and available) to prepare and transmit the message. How urgent is the message? Are there time differences (eg in international communication) that will dictate when the message should be sent or received (or the use of a medium that will minimise the problem, such as fax or e-mail which can be received out of hours).

(ii) The **complexity of the message**. What communication media will enable it to be most readily understood (for example, adding diagrams or maps)?

(iii) Whether or not a **written record is required**, for example to confirm instructions or provide legal evidence of contract terms.

(iv) Whether or not there is a need for **interaction or 'real time'** exchange of information: question and answer, instant feedback and so on.

(v) Whether there is a **need for confidentiality** (such as private interview or personal letter) or, conversely, the wide and swift dissemination of information (such as by open meeting or notice board).

(vi) Sensitivity to the **effect of the message** on the recipient: the need for tact, personal involvement (eg in a face-to-face interview) or impersonality (eg in a formal letter), for example.

(vii) The cost of preparing and sending the message, in relation to all the above, for the most effective communication at justifiable expense.

46 ORAL AND NON-VERBAL SKILLS

> **Tutor's hint.** Listening and non-verbal skills are fairly straightforward. The wording of the question suggests that you should make some effort to format your answer as draft guidelines or advice, rather than in the third person ('managers should...'). Remember that while listening is a receiving skill, 'effectiveness as a non-verbal communicator' includes both the receiving and the giving of non-verbal cues: ensure that you cover both aspects in your answer.

(a)

> **GUIDELINES: HOW TO BE AN EFFECTIVE LISTENER**
>
> - **Be ready**. Get your attitude right at the start and decide to listen. You might be able to do some background research or other preparation to provide a context for the message you are to receive.
>
> - **Be interested**. Don't try to soak up a message passively and then be surprised to find it dull: *make* it interesting by asking questions: how can I use this information? How is it relevant to me?
>
> - **Be patient**. Try not to interrupt, however much you disagree or wish to add relevant input: wait for a suitable opening, and do not let the planning of your response distract you from listening to the message.
>
> - **Keep your mind open**. Be aware of any negative reactions to the speaker's message, delivery or appearance: don't let them get in the way of hearing accurately.
>
> - **Keep your mind going**. Being open-minded does not mean uncritical acceptance. Use your critical faculties: test the speaker's assumptions, logic and evidence, and your own interpretations.
>
> - **Keep your mind on the job**. Concentrate. Do not get side-tracked by irrelevancies: co-operate with the speaker in getting to the point of the message. Listen for main points, summary and conclusion.
>
> - **Give feedback**. Encourage the speaker and check your own understanding by giving feedback in the form of non-verbal cues. If there are opportunities, ask for confirmation, explanation or more information as required.
>
> - **Use non-verbal cues**. Be aware of the sub-text given by gestures, facial expressions, tone of voice and so on.

(b)

GUIDELINES: HOW TO BE AN EFFECTIVE NON-VERBAL COMMUNICATOR

Be aware of the variety of non-verbal cues that can send messages: body language, posture, proximity, gestures, facial expressions, sounds and silences.

Be aware of the variety of meanings and uses of non-verbal cues: adding emphasis, confirming or undermining verbal messages.

Be aware of your own non-verbal behaviours, and control them in order to:

- Provide appropriate feedback to the sender of a message

- Project the desired image

- Establish the desired atmosphere or effect (eg rapport or empathy)

- Reinforce or add emphasis to your spoken messages

Be aware of the non-verbal behaviours of others, and interpret them in order to:

- Receive helpful feedback from your listener and modify your message accordingly

- Recognise underlying feelings and sub-texts, where words are constrained by formalities or the need for disguise

- Read situations in order to modify your own communication and response strategy.

Seek feedback while communicating, and from trusted colleagues and mentors, to appraise the effect and effectiveness of your non-verbal style.

---

47   COUNSELLING

Tutor's hint. This should be fairly straightforward, if you are on top of the material: don't underestimate the possibility that you will have to answer questions on what may seem like comparatively 'minor' syllabus topics. Remember that you have to answer four questions out of five in this section of the exam!

(a)   **Purposes of counselling in an organisation**

The Institute of Personnel Development issued a Statement on Counselling in the Workplace in 1992 which makes it clear that effective counselling is not merely a matter of 'pastoral' care for individuals (although it does embrace that, where required), but is very much in the organisation's business interests.

(i)   Appropriate use of counselling can **prevent under-performance** and reduce labour turnover and absenteeism.

(ii)   Effective counselling **demonstrates an organisation's commitment** to and concern for its employees and so may improve staff loyalty and commitment.

(iii)   The **development of employees is of value to the organisation,** and effective counselling may give employees the confidence and problem-solving skills necessary to take responsibility for self-development and for other organisation objectives.

(iv)   Workplace counselling recognises that **the organisation may be contributing to its employees' problems,** and therefore provides an opportunity to reassess organisational policies and practices and to stimulate feedback and discussion on performance.

(b)   **The DOs and DON'Ts of workplace counselling**

Counselling is not the same as coaching or advising. 'It is a way of relating and responding to another person so that that person is helped to explore his thoughts, feelings and behaviour with the aim of reaching a clearer understanding.' (Rees)

- DO ensure time, privacy, non-interruption and as non-stressful an environment as possible for the session

- DO guarantee confidentiality unless the counsellee gives permission for aspects of the discussion to be disclosed for specific purposes (such as follow-up action)

- DO establish rapport ('pace') before challenging, questioning or offering information or advice ('leading')

- DO demonstrate empathy (by reflecting back, summarising, giving feedback, being sensitive to the counsellee's beliefs/values/context/vocabulary and so on)

- DO listen actively (showing interest, using non-verbal cues of attention, checking understanding)

- DON'T be judgemental, take sides or apply your own feelings/values to the counsellee or the situation

- DON'T give advice or solutions: even if your style is more directive, your role is to empower, not to fix or rescue

- DON'T self-disclose (share your own problems or solutions) unless necessary to inspire trust and openness

- DON'T sympathise (join the counsellee in negative thoughts/feelings/behaviours): empathise instead

- DO accept and affirm the person, but DON'T accept or affirm behaviours which are damaging to that person or others: be soft on the person, hard on the problem

48   IDEOLOGIES OF CONFLICT

> **Tutor's hint.** This is an interesting question. If you weren't familiar with the 'happy family', 'evolutionary', 'conflict', 'unitary', 'pluralist' or 'radical' views of conflict, you should still have been able to argue three viewpoints in part (a) from the suggestions given in the introduction to the question. For example: conflict is an inevitable evil in organisations; conflict is bad, but exceptional in organisations; conflict is a constructive force in organisational survival and growth. Part (b) expands on some of these issues: the view that conflict can be good or bad according to how it is managed is perhaps the most common and useful for management.

(a)   **Three basic viewpoints on conflict**

(i)   A **unitary** ideology of conflict (sometimes called the 'happy family view') presents organisations as co-operative structures in which conflict is not natural. All members of the organisation, despite their different roles, have common objectives and values which unite their efforts. The prerogative of management is accepted as paternal and in everyone's best interests. Conflicts are exceptional and arise primarily from misunderstandings, personality factors, inflexible expectations and factors outside the organisation's control. Effective management should eliminate conflict by strong culture, good multi-directional communication, collaborative goal-setting and motivational leadership.

(ii)   A **pluralist** ideology (or 'conflict view') of conflict presents organisations as political coalitions of individuals and groups which have their own interests and are in competition for limited resources, status, rewards and so on. Management has to create a workable structure for collaboration, taking into account the objectives of all the various stakeholders in the organisation. A mutual survival strategy, involving the control of conflict through compromise, can be made acceptable in varying degrees to all concerned. The pluralist viewpoint also allows for an '*evolutionary view*', which suggests that conflict is a useful basis for evolutionary change: it keeps the organisation sensitive to the need for change, while reinforcing its essential framework of control and balancing competing interests.

(iii) A **radical** ideology of conflict argues that there is an inequality of power between the controllers of economic resources (shareholders and managers) and those who depend on access to those resources (wage earners). Those in power exploit the others by indoctrinating them to accept the legitimacy of their rights to power, and thus perpetuate the system. Conflict in the radical view does not aim for mutual survival or evolutionary change, but for revolutionary change: bringing down an unjust system.

(**BPP note**. You might consider hostility to globalisation as an example of this.)

(b)   **Constructive and destructive effects of conflict**

Conflict can be constructive when its effect is to:

- Introduce different solutions to problems
- Define power relationships more clearly
- Encourage creativity through the testing and challenging of ideas
- Focus attention on individual contributions
- Bring emotions out into the open, where they can be resolved
- Enforce a 'reality check' on complacent or ill-thought out plans

Conflict can be destructive when its effect is to:

- Distract attention from the task
- Polarise views and create entrenched and blinkered responses to problems
- Subvert task objectives in favour of secondary goals
- Encourage defensive or negative behaviours and political game-playing
- Stimulate emotional win-lose conflicts (hostility)
- Disintegrate work groups

49   DISCIPLINARY ACTION

> **Tutor's hint.** The crucial point to note is that the manager (as described in the micro-scenario of the question) seems to associate 'discipline' with 'punishment'. The basis for your answer will therefore be your understanding that discipline is a positive concept, involving problem-solving and empowering improved behaviour or performance in future. Note in part (c) that you are asked for principles related to 'interpersonal aspects', not procedures.

(a)   **Discipline**

Discipline can be considered as a condition in an enterprise in which there is orderliness, in which individuals and teams behave responsibly in accordance with the values and goals of the organisation and accepted norms. It is not merely about the use or threat of punishment for infringements of organisational rules and standards.

'**Negative' discipline is based on the threat of sanctions**. Even so, it is not primarily designed to be punitive (punishing an offence), but to **encourage people to choose to behave in the desired way**, as a **deterrent** (warning people not to behave in undesirable ways) or **reformative** (encouraging offenders not to reoffend).

In a general sense, 'discipline' is positive in so far as it reflects the willing co-operation of individuals in the shared goals and values of the enterprise. It is a key element of 'esprit de corps'.

(b) **Disciplinary situations**

Disciplinary situations may arise in any number of contexts

(i) Law and **regulation in the country** in which the organisation operates (for example, sexual harassment or physical violence against a fellow employee, theft of organisational property, or the breaking of health and safety rules).

(ii) The organisation's **own rules and regulations** (for example, persistent breaking of rules regarding start, finish and break times, non-smoking areas and so on).

(iii) The organisation's **performance standards** and targets (for example, persistently excessive rates of errors or customer complaints).

(iv) **Supervisors' assessment of behaviour as unacceptable** within the organisation's culture and expectations (for example, absenteeism beyond an acceptable frequency and/or without acceptable justification, or open insubordination).

(v) **Situations arising outside the workplace which impact** on the employee's behaviour or performance at work (for example, drug or alcohol abuse).

(c) **Five principles for managing the interpersonal aspects of disciplinary action**

(i) **Immediacy.** After noting the offence, the manager should proceed to take disciplinary action as speedily as possible, subject to the investigations that may need to be made, and avoiding haste and on-the-spot emotions.

(ii) **Advance warning.** All employees should know in advance (eg via the Staff Handbook) what is expected of them and what the rules and regulations are.

(iii) **Consistency.** Each time an infraction occurs, appropriate disciplinary action should be taken, without the unpredictability of favouritism or 'making examples' of particular individuals.

(iv) **Impersonality.** Penalties should be connected with the offence and not based on personalities. Once disciplinary action has been taken, no grudges should be borne.

(v) **Privacy.** Unless the manager's authority is challenged directly and in public, disciplinary action should be taken in private, to avoid the spread of conflict and the humiliation (or martyrdom) of the employee concerned.

50   GRIEVANCE INTERVIEW

> **Tutor's hint.** This should be straightforward as long as you noted the introduction to the question and correctly distinguished 'grievance' from 'discipline' and as long as you paid attention to the topic keywords 'grievance *interview*' (in part (a)) and 'matters that should be stated' and 'policy' (part (b)).

(a) **Grievance interview**

The subordinate wants a positive result from the grievance interview, which the manager may or may not be able to give. Prior to the interview, the manager should have some idea of the complaint and its possible source. The meeting itself can then proceed through three main phases.

(i) **Exploration.** The manager should try to gather as much information as possible on the problem: its background, the facts, the causes (manifest and hidden). At this stage, the manager should not attempt to offer interpretations or solutions: the subordinate must feel thoroughly heard and understood, and the outcome must be seen not to be pre-judged.

(ii) **Consideration.** The manager has three essential tasks.

- Check the facts.

- Analyse the causes – the problem of which the complaint may be only a symptom.

- Evaluate options for responding to the complaint and the implications of any response made.

It may be that information can be given to clear up a misunderstanding, or the employee will – having aired his or her feelings – withdraw the formal complaint. However, the meeting may have to be adjourned (say, for 48 hours) while the manager gets extra information, considers both sides and evaluates other response options.

(iii) **Reply.** The manager, having reached and reviewed his conclusions, reconvenes the meeting to convey (and justify, if required) his decision, hear counter-arguments and appeals. The outcome (agreed or disagreed) should be recorded in writing.

Follow-up action will need to be carried through as agreed and minuted in the interview. Further interviews – for conflict resolution or counselling – may be included in this action.

(b) **Matters that should be stated in a formal grievance policy**

(i) What grades of employee are entitled to pursue a particular type of grievance

(ii) Employees' rights in each type of grievance

(iii) What the procedures for pursuing a grievance should be, including: whom to approach in the first instance. Who will conduct investigations and interviews; in what circumstances appeals can be made and to whom

(iv) The rights of the employee to be accompanied by a colleague, trade union or staff association representative

(v) Time limits for initiating certain grievance procedures and subsequent stages of them

(vi) The requirement for written records of all meetings to be made and distributed to concerned parties.

Managing People
BPP Mock Exam 1:
December 2001

Question Paper:	
Time allowed	3 hours
This paper is divided into two sections	
Section A	This question is compulsory and MUST be attempted
Section B	FOUR questions ONLY to be answered

Disclaimer of liability

Please note that we have based our predictions of the content of the December 2001 exam on our long experience of the ACCA exams. We do not claim to have any endorsement of the predictions from either the examiner or the ACCA and we do not guarantee that either the specific questions, or the general areas, that are forecast will necessarily be included in the exams, in part or in whole.

We do not accept any liability or responsibility to any person who takes, or does not take, any action based (either in whole or in part and either directly or indirectly) upon any statement or omission made in this book. We encourage students to study all topics in the ACCA syllabus and the mock exam in this book is intended as an aid to revision only.

paper 1.3

DO NOT OPEN THIS PAPER UNTIL YOU ARE READY TO START

UNDER EXAMINATION CONDITIONS

Section A - This section is compulsory and MUST be attempted

1   Sandra Kristensson, Finance Manager of GBH Ltd, has noticed a marked decrease in the accounts department's efficiency in the last few months.

The problems appear to coincide with the introduction of the 'Employee of the Month' competition, the recruiting of a new supervisor with a rather abrasive personal style and discussions over the re-allocation of office space. There has been no overt argument over these issues: indeed, staff appear to be communicating less and less.

GBH has recently appointed you as assistant Human Resource Manager. Sandra Kristensson has asked you to help her diagnose and resolve the problems in her department.

Required:

(a) Explain what you think may be happening in the accounts department and why.

(10 marks)

(b) Draft notes on the tactics commonly used in conflict situations:

(i)   by the conflicting parties   (5 marks)
(ii)   by managers responding to the conflict   (7 marks)

(c) Explain how you would go about managing the conflict in the accounts department.   (10 marks)

(d) Explain how the conflict in the accounts department may be seen as constructive or positive in its results.   (8 marks)

(40 marks)

Section B – Answer any FOUR questions. ALL questions carry equal marks.

2   Modern complex organisations and dynamic environments require both organisations and individuals to accept the need for lifelong continuous learning. Your organisation has accepted this idea and requires advice on how to improve learning within the organisation.

Required:

(a) Explain the term 'learning organisation'.   (3 marks)

(b) Explain any four characteristics of a learning organisation.   (8 marks)

(c) Identify four likely barriers to learning which might be found in an organisation.

    (4 marks)

(15 marks)

3   You have been asked to advise the accounts manager on the documentation required for the recruitment of a new accounts assistant.

Required:

(a) Briefly explain the difference between a job description and a person specification.   (4 marks)

(b) Describe the contents of a job description.   (5 marks)

(c) Outline the uses and limitations of job descriptions.   (6 marks)

(15 marks)

4   Your organisation has decided to implement a radical programme of empowerment, but its managers and subordinates alike are unclear as to how delegation works. You have been asked to give a practical presentation on delegation skills.

Required:

(a) Describe the process of delegation.   (5 marks)

(b) Identify the factors to be taken into account in the decision:

    (i)   when to delegate a decision to a subordinate   (5 marks)

    (ii)   when to refer a decision upwards to a superior   (5 marks)

(15 marks)

5   As part of your training, you have been sent on a leadership development course. On your return, your manager has asked you to report on what you have learned in the following areas.

Required:

(a) Describe Blake and Mouton's managerial grid.   (5 marks)

(b) Identify the four extreme scores highlighted by Blake and Mouton.   (4 marks)

(c) Evaluate the usefulness of the managerial grid to an organisation.   (6 marks)

(15 marks)

6   The staff association representatives in your organisation have heard that management are proposing to implement 'performance management' as an alternative to traditional appraisal. They do not know what it involves. You have been asked to explain.

Required:

(a) Briefly define and describe the process of 'performance management'.

(10 marks)

(b) List the advantages to employees of the organisation adopting a performance management approach.   (5 marks)

(15 marks)

ANSWERS

DO NOT TURN THIS PAGE UNTIL YOU
HAVE COMPLETED THE MOCK EXAM

WARNING! APPLYING THE BPP MARKING SCHEME

If you decide to mark your paper using the BPP marking scheme, you should bear in mind the following points.

1   The BPP solutions are not definitive: you will see that we have applied the marking scheme to our solutions to show how good answers should gain marks, but there may be more than one way to answer the question. You must try to judge fairly whether different points made in your answers are correct and relevant and therefore worth marks according to our marking scheme.

2   If you have a friend or colleague who is studying or has studied this paper, you might ask him or her to mark your paper for you, thus gaining a more objective assessment. Remember you and your friend are not trained or objective markers, so try to avoid complacency or pessimism if you appear to have done very well or very badly.

3   You should be aware that BPP's answers are longer than you would be expected to write. Sometimes, therefore, you would gain the same number of marks for making the basic point as we have shown as being available for a slightly more detailed or extensive solution.

It is most important that you analyse your solutions in detail and that you attempt to be as objective as possible.

PLAN OF ATTACK

Managing People is a 'wordy' subject, without the clear 'yes' and 'no' answers you can achieve in the other papers at this level. That doesn't mean that you can waffle your way to a pass in your sleep, but there are plenty of easy marks to be had.

The keys to passing this paper are:

- Using the knowledge you have – you can't rely on 'common sense'; the questions are often factual, and the scenario will expect you to apply theory and background knowledge.

- Time management – Section A should take 72 minutes, maximum and each of the section B questions should take 27 minutes. (So, if you start Section A at 2pm, you should have finished at 3.12pm.)

- Clear presentation of your answers

Read the rubric. You must do question A, and you have to do four out of five questions in Section B. So your **only** choices are:

- The **order** in which you do the questions

- Which **one** of the Section B questions you **don't** want to do

Looking through **this paper**, Section A covers conflict within a department – which you will need to diagnose in more depth, and Section B offers a variety of questions covering organisation (question 2), human resources management (questions 3 and 6, on job descriptions and performance management, including appraisals, respectively), and management skills (question 4 on delegation and question 5 on leadership).

In this paper should you do Section A first?

ONLY if you're VERY comfortable – YES, get it out of the way, in no more than 72 minutes bearing in mind that part (a) should take 18 minutes, part (b) in total 21 minutes, part (c) 18 minutes and part (d) 13 minutes. So, if you start part (a) at 2pm, you should have finished it by 3.12pm at the latest, and hence completing your Section B selection questions at 3.39, 4.06, 4.33 and 5pm at the latest.

So how should you tackle Section A? We've already talked about time management, and we strongly recommend that you do the different parts of this question in order. In part (a) - well, you know there is conflict, and you can deduce some contentious issues, perhaps supported with relevant theory. It is not enough to repeat the question, by the way. Part (b) asks for theory, and parts (c) and (d) ask you to offer practical advice for the accounts department.

If you don't want to do Section A first... in **this** paper, Section A requires you to diagnose a situation, and deduce facts from it. It then covers conflict and its implications. So, in our view, it isn't the friendliest scenario question you could be given, certainly if you compare it to the pilot paper, given the need for interpretation.

Another reason for leaving Section A in **this** paper until the end is that the section B questions may jog your memory about some of the issues in section A.

The Section B questions are relatively straightforward, requiring some factual explanation followed by some work evaluating the topic. So your choice of your least favourite section B question will by and large be determined by your revision. In short, your choice is what to leave out. If you're comfortable with HRM, do questions 3 and 6; if you're comfortable with management, do questions 4 and 5. Question 2 on the learning organisation is probably the 'odd one out' as it has little interconnections with the rest of the paper and is unlikely to give you fresh ideas.

If you do **Section** B first, you will start your first question at 2pm, finishing at 2.27, and completing the other questions at 2.54, 3.21, and 3.48, leaving you 72 minutes to complete Section A by 5pm. **And remember the mark allocation reflects the time you should spend. Looking at the HRM questions,** question 3 seems utterly straightforward, whereas you might need a bit more imagination for question 6. For the management questions, question 4 requires a bit of imagination, but for question 5 you need to be sure of the detail of Blake and Mouton's grid so perhaps this is a bit riskier.

1   CONFLICT AT GBH LTD

> **Tutor's hint.** The questions set should have given you a fairly clear hint as to what the scenario was meant to portray. Once you realised this was a conflict question, there should be plenty of ammunition for part (a): there are classic conflict issues of intra-team competition, personality clashes and competition for limited status symbols and resources. You might note that conflict can exist without 'overt' displays of hostility such as argument, and that loss of communication is an indicator of possible underlying conflict. In part (c), you will need to address each of the causes you identified in part (a): you may choose to take a comprehensive 'ecology'-based approach, or to discuss a specific win-win conflict resolution process. (We have used elements of both, for your revision.)

(a) **Analysis of the situation in the GBH accounts department**

It appears that there is underlying conflict within the department. The fact that this is not emerging as overt argument is not an indication to the contrary, since conflict can be very subtle and submerged. The withdrawal of co-operation manifested in decreased communication and emerging inefficiencies is sufficient to investigate the possibility of conflict further.

The current situation in the accounts department presents a number of **classic causes** of conflict.

(i) **The introduction of the 'Employee of the Month' competition has certainly provided potential for conflict, particularly since no such attempt to compare individual performance has previously been used. This may have created a perception that management is carrying out some kind of selection process for promotion or (once insecurities grow out of proportion) even redundancy.**

Deutsch reported a classic experiment in which students were given puzzles to work at in two different styles of group: 'co-operative' groups were told that the grade each individual got at the end of the course would depend on the performance of the group; 'competitive' groups were told that each student would receive a grade according to his own contributions. The co-operative groups, compared with the competitive ones, had greater productivity, better quality of output and discussion, better co-ordination and work sharing and better relationships.

(ii) The **directly competitive element discussed above has been reinforced by the more 'political' competition between department members for prime office space.** In any department, there will be some competition for scarce resources (including space, window area and so on): **office space** is particularly powerful in political game-playing, however, because **it symbolises the status and worth of the individual in the organisation.** Some of the insecurities of the Employee of the Month rivalry - and what it may be used to prove – may be exaggerating the importance of the office re-allocation.

(iii) **The reportedly abrasive personal style of the new supervisor is likely, in this highly-charged climate, to create interpersonal conflict and perhaps further insecurity about the way the department is being changed.** Personality clashes are in themselves a source of irritation and hostility, and can cause resistance in the team which would help to explain the reduction of communication: withholding information is an application of negative power.

The above is, of course, partly speculation on the basis of the evidence available. It would certainly be worth having an informal discussion with individual members of the team to get a sense of their perception of the situation in the department to confirm or deny the conflict hypothesis.

(b) **Tactics used in the conflict situation**

Common tactics used by conflicting parties

- **Withholding** information from one another, since 'knowledge is power'.

- **Distorting information**. This will enable the individual presenting the information to manipulate the recipients and perhaps manoeuvre them into difficulties.

- **Empire building**. A group (especially a specialist group, as in accounting) which considers its influence to be neglected might seek to impose rules, procedures or restrictions on other groups, in order to increase their power.

- **Informal organisation**. Individuals and groups seek to by-pass formal channels of communication and decision-making by establishing informal contacts and coalitions with people in positions of influence.

- **Fault-finding** with the work of others: trying to prove rivals wrong, or to damage their position of influence or trust.

Tactics used by management in response to conflict

- **Denial/withdrawal**: 'sweeping it under the carpet'. If the conflict is trivial, ignoring it until it 'blows over' may be sufficient, but underlying causes can blow conflict up to unmanageable proportions.

- **Suppression**: 'smoothing over', to preserve working relationships. Some cracks, however, cannot be papered over.

- **Dominance**: the application of power or influence to settle the issue. The disadvantage of this is in setting up winners and losers.

- **Compromise**: bargaining, negotiating, conciliating. To some extent this will be inevitable, but it can polarise positions (in order to allow for eventual compromise) and can be seen as a weak solution to a problem.

- **Integration/collaboration**: subordinating the needs of individuals to the requirements of the task. Individuals must accept the need to modify their views for the sake of the task, and group effort must be seen to be superior to individual effort.

- **Encourage co-operative behaviours**: setting goals for all teams/departments, establishing joint problem-solving teams and so on.

(c) **Managing the conflict in the GBH accounts department**

There are a number of approaches to the conflict (if such it is found to be on investigation).

'Ecological' strategies are aimed at creating conditions which facilitate co-operation and positive interpersonal relations. For example:

(i) Reinforcing the 'team' nature of the department, and its shared objectives, through direct communication, supervisory style and team-based recognitions and rewards (over and above the 'Employee of the Month scheme).

(ii) Encouraging more (and more open) communication in all directions: more regular departmental meetings, informal contacts, management by walking around and so on.

(iii)   Minimising political gameplaying. We may, for example, consider allocating offices by ballot, or taking the seriousness out of the 'Employee of the Month' competition so it becomes good-humoured.

Handy also discussed '**regulation**' strategies for controlling conflict where it is likely to arise. One such strategy, which could be applied in our case, is the provision of conflict **resolution counselling**, and (if necessary) arbitration of disputes. We may start with some informal counselling of the new supervisor and those who have a grievance because of his style.)

Conflict can most constructively be managed with a belief in the possibility of a 'win-win' solution, in which nobody 'loses': even if such a solution is ultimately impracticable, the effort to find it (by motivated communication and co-operative problem-solving) may in itself resolve the conflict in a creative way. It is recommended to have a meeting (facilitated according to 'win-win' guidelines) on the issue of office space. It may be that different people actually want or fear different outcomes: needing more natural light, say, or proximity to equipment, or fearing that 'missing out' on an office means losing status in the department. Once these motivations are out in the open, it may be possible to find alternative solutions to each of the expressed needs or fears.

(d)   **Constructive conflict**

Conflict can be highly positive, in any context, where its effect is to:

- Introduce different solutions to problems
- Define power relationships and limits more clearly
- Encourage creativity by testing ideas
- Improve the quality of decisions by challenging them
- Focus attention on individual contributions
- Bring emotions out into the open where they can be resolved

In the current situation at GBH, the conflicts may have some of these positive effects.

(i)   **They have highlighted the fact that staff are not motivated by the new supervisor's abrasive style.** This can now be dealt with by counselling the supervisor, although it may be that the team's resistance is sufficient feedback to motivate him to change his style, once it becomes clear that it is not effective in creating a motivated or performing team.

(ii)   **The Employee of the Month competition has stimulated some genuine extra performance,** dispute the negative consequences for co-operative team-working. It may be that, if individual effort is recognised and reinforced, and people feel less threatened by comparison, competitiveness will subside into more constructive competition.

(iii)   **The conflict for priority in office space has highlighted some genuine issues of concern about current office facilities which can now be addressed.** It has also highlighted some personal insecurities about status and recognition in the department, symbolised by prime office locations: these issues of motivation and morale need to be dealt with at a deeper level so that staff feel secure and appreciated without political point-scoring.

(iv)   The practice of conflict has brought out some interpersonal differences within the team which, having been identified, can be constructively managed to improve our appreciation of diversity and teamworking skills.

2   THE LEARNING ORGANISATION

> **Tutor's hint.** 'Learning organisation' may seem like a comparatively small topic – but it is highly fashionable and relevant to key organisational issues such as flexibility and change management. In part (c), you may have chosen to base your answer on Peter Senge's 'learning disabilities' or any other relevant framework.

(a)   **The learning organisation**

The learning organisation has been defined as **'an organisation that facilitates the learning of all its members and continuously transforms itself'**.

The purpose of these processes is to create an organisational structure and culture that is capable of adapting and developing, without trauma, to the changing environment and the changing demands of all the (internal and external) stakeholders of the organisations.

The key dimensions of the learning organisation are: the generation and transfer of knowledge; a tolerance for risk and failure as learning opportunities; and a systematic, on-going, collective and scientific approach to problem-solving.

(b)   **Four characteristics of a learning organisation**

Garvin suggests that learning organisations are good at five things: systematic problem-solving, experimentation, learning from past experience, learning from others and transferring knowledge through the organisation.

   (i)   **Experimentation.** Learning organisations systematically search for and test new knowledge. Decision-making is based on 'hypothesis-generating, hypothesis-testing' techniques: the plan-do-check-act cycle. Application of information and learning is key. Innovation is encouraged, with a tolerance for risk.

   (ii)   **Learning from past experience.** Learning organisations freely seek and provide feedback on performance and processes: they review their successes and failures, assess them systematically and communicate lessons to all employees. Mistakes and failures are regarded as learning opportunities.

   (iii)   **Learning from others.** Learning organisations recognise that the most powerful insights and opportunities come from looking 'outside the box' of the immediate environment. They encourage employees to seek information and learning opportunities outside the organisation as well as inside.

   (iv)   **Transferring knowledge quickly and efficiently throughout the organisation.** Information is made available at all levels and across functional boundaries. Education, training and networking opportunities are constantly available.

(c)   **Four likely barriers to learning**

   (i)   **'I am my position'.** Individuals focus on the task they perform rather than the purposes they fulfil, or what their job is *for*: they tend to think within the boundaries of their position.

   (ii)   **'The enemy is out there'.** Individuals shift the blame for problems and failures to someone or something else, rather than taking responsibility for problem-solving.

   (iii)   **'The fixation on events'.** Organisational thinking is dominated by past and current events, rather than longer-term patterns of change: trends, threats, opportunities, possibilities and so on.

(iv)   **'The parable of the boiled frog.'** Individuals and organisations fail to perceive and respond to gradually-building threats to their survival: they only notice sudden, drastic changes, to which they respond in crisis.

3   JOB DESCRIPTIONS AND PERSON SPECIFICATIONS

> **Tutor's hint.** Job analysis, job description and person specification are the bread and butter of exam questions on recruitment and selection: make sure you can define and distinguish between the terms (correctly!) and that you have a good grasp of the basics like process or content, uses and limitations. Don't get complacent when you encounter a question you know lots about, however: you need all the more to pay attention to mark allocation and related time allocation.

(a)   **Difference between a job description and a person specification**

A **job description** is a profile of the job or (in the context of recruitment) of the vacancy to be filled. A **person specification** (or personnel specification) is a profile of the kind of person the organisation should recruit or develop for a given job or vacancy: it sets out the attributes a job holder requires to perform a job satisfactorily.

The difference between the two documents is basically that a person specification focuses on the qualities of the person which will fulfil the requirements of a position, while the job description focuses on the requirements themselves: one is person-centred, the other job-centred. In addition, the person specification involves the organisation's aspirations for an 'ideal' or 'desirable' level of performance in the job, while the job description describes tasks and responsibilities.

(b)   **Content of a job description**

- Job title and department.

- Reporting relationships: the person to whom the job holder is responsible.

- Job summary: outlining the major functions and tools, machinery and special equipment used.

- Job content: a list of the tasks or duties that constitute the job, including degrees of difficulty or responsibility involved.

- The extent (and limits) of the jobholder's authority and accountabilities.

- The relation of the job to other positions, including superior and subordinate positions and liaison with other departments.

- Working terms and conditions (hours, pay rates, special conditions of the job), development opportunities and so on.

(c)   **Uses and limitation of job descriptions**

Job descriptions are most commonly used in the following circumstances.

(i)   In recruitment, to define the skills and qualifications required by the vacancy, as a basis for screening, interviewing and testing applicants.

(ii)   In job evaluation, for establishing wage rates.

(iii)   In induction, training, appraisal and development: to highlight the scope and functions of the job, training needs, lines of potential development and so on.

Townsend (*Up the Organisation*) suggested that **job descriptions are of limited use.**

(i) They are only suited for jobs where the work is largely repetitive and predictable.

(ii) Management jobs are likely to be constantly changing as external influences impact upon them, so a job description is constantly out of date.

(iii) Difficulties arise when job descriptions are taken too literally, and cause demarcation disputes and costly over-manning practices.

A job description is a static 'snapshot' of a job at a given time: it requires flexibility and constant, negotiated revision. It must also be remembered that job descriptions are 'the map' – not 'the territory': they are designed as a tool for management, not a constraint.

4   DELEGATION

> **Tutor's hint.** Do not be distracted by the micro-scenario's mention of a presentation. You could be creative in formatting your answer if you wish, but the basic marks still have to be earned by solid content. You may not have thought about delegation from the subordinates' point of view, in which case part (b) (ii) on 'upwards delegation' may have been a challenge.

(a)   **The process of delegation**

Delegation of authority occurs when a superior gives to a subordinate part of his or her own authority to carry out actions or make decisions.

Step 1: Specify the expected performance levels of the assistant, keeping in mind the assistant's level of expertise.

Step 2: Formally assign tasks to the assistant, who should formally undertake to perform them.

Step 3: Allocate resources and authority to the assistant to enable him or her to carry out the delegated tasks to the expected level of performance.

Step 4: Maintain contact with the assistant to review the progress made and to give constructive feedback.

It should be remembered that the ultimate responsibility and accountability for the task remains with the delegator.

(b)   **Factors to consider in deciding when to delegate**

There is a natural 'trust-control' dilemma (Handy) in delegation, which may pose real difficulties in delegating authority. Some of the factors to consider are as follows.

(i) Is the **acceptance of a decision by subordinates required** for morale, working relationships and/or effective implementation of the decision?

(ii) Is the **quality of the decision important,** and does the supervisor alone have the information or experience to make it effectively?

(iii) Is the **expertise or experience of subordinates relevant** or necessary to the task, such that the quality of the decision will be enhanced?

(iv) Can **trust** be placed in the competence and reliability of the subordinates to exercise delegated authority?

(v) Does the decision require **tact and confidentiality,** or, on the other hand, maximum exposure and assimilation by employees?

(vi) Is the **supervisor overloaded with tasks,** while subordinates who are capable of exercising authority are under-utilised?

(vii) Does the culture and practice of the organisation positively or negatively regard and reinforce delegation?

(c) **Factors to consider in deciding when to refer upwards**

In instances where 'upward delegation' may be necessary, the subordinate should consider the following.

(i) Whether the decision is relevant to the superior: will it have any impact on his or her area of responsibility, such as strategy, staffing or control action?

(ii) Whether the superior has authority or information relevant to the decision that the subordinate does not possess: for example, authority to liaise with other departments.

(iii) The politics and culture of the organisation: will the superior expect to be consulted, or will the subordinate be regarded as weak if the decision is referred upwards?

5   BLAKE AND MOUTON

Tutor's hint. Blake and Mouton's managerial grid is only one model of leadership style, but it is accessible and popular in management development. The challenge of this question is to describe the grid (part (a)) *without* pre-empting your discussion of the four extreme scores (part (b)). We have chosen to use a diagram in our answer to part (a), showing the four extreme scores without further discussion – and allowing us to identify them in part (b) without having to describe their location. Part (c) offers a useful lesson: get used to thinking critically and practically about the theories you encounter in your studies.

(a) **Blake and Mouton's Managerial Grid**

Robert Blake and Jane Mouton suggested that there are two basic dimensions of leadership: concern for production (or task performance) and concern for people. Along each of these two dimensions, managers can be located at any point on a continuum from very low to very high concern.

Blake and Mouton modeled these permutations as 'the Managerial Grid'. One axis represents concern for people and the other, concern for production, with nine 'points' on each axis. A questionnaire was designed to enable users to analyse and plot the 'positions' of individual respondents on the grid.

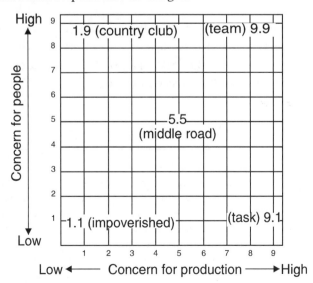

(b) **Four extreme scores**

The four extreme scores (identified on the diagram above) are as follows.

(i) *1.1 (impoverished management):* low concern for production and people. The manager does not greatly care whether the team is motivated and satisfied, nor whether any more than minimal task performance is achieved.

(ii) *1.9 (country club):* low concern for production, high concern for people. The manager seeks the satisfaction of staff needs and the preservation of relationships even at the expense of task performance.

(iii) *9.1 (task management):* high concern for the task, low concern for people. The manager concentrates on achieving results, even at the expense of staff and team maintenance needs.

(iv) *9.9 (team management):* high concern for the task and people. The manager recognises that work goals can most effectively be achieved by integrating them with individual and team goals and by encouraging staff development.

(c) **The usefulness of the managerial grid**

The grid was intended as an appraisal and management development tool. It recognises that a balance is required between concern for the task and concern for people, and that a high degree of both is possible (and highly effective) at the same time.

The grid thus offers a number of useful insights for the identification of management training and development needs. It shows in an easily assimilated form where the habitual behaviours and assumptions of a given manager may exhibit a lack of balance between the dimensions and/or a low degree of concern in either dimension or both.

However, the grid is a simplified model and as such as practical limitations.

(i) **It assumes that 9.9 is the desirable model for effective leadership**. In some contexts, this may not necessarily be so. Where there is high unemployment or heavy automation, for example, concern for people may not be a priority.

(ii) **It is open to oversimplification**. Scores can appear polarised, with judgements attached about managers' suitability or performance.

(iii) **Organisational context and culture**, technology and other 'givens' (Handy) influence the manager's style of leadership as well as the two dimensions covered by the grid.

(iv) **Any managerial theory is only useful in so far as it is useable in practice by managers:** if the grid is only used to inform managers that they 'must acquire greater concern for the task', against their context and inclinations, it will only result in stress and inconsistent behaviour.

6   PERFORMANCE MANAGEMENT

> **Tutor's hint.** This is straightforward, as long as you remember (accurately) what performance management is: because it is a mixture of management by objectives and performance appraisal, there may be a potential pitfall here. Once you have defined *and* outlined the process of performance management in part (a), the advantages to employees - and the staff representatives to whom you are explaining them in this micro-scenario - should be fairly obvious. Check that you read 'employ*ees*' and not 'employers' or 'the organisation'. (Look out for this in the exam: you don't get marks for a good answer to the wrong question!)

(a) **Definition and process of performance management**

Performance management is an approach to performance appraisal and development which is designed to integrate individual, team and organisational goals in order to facilitate both employee commitment and business performance. It is based on 'understanding and managing performance within an agreed framework of planned goals, standards and competence requirements' (Armstrong). An alternative to the infrequent, retrospective and potentially judgemental process of performance appraisal, performance management is the basis for on-going, collaborative, positive and result-oriented improvement and development planning.

The process of performance management may be described as five steps.

Step1: **Identify and describe key functions, competencies, targets and standards required for job performance.** This should be derived from the goals and objectives set out for the performance unit, which in turn should be derived from the corporate plan of the business as a whole.

Step 2: **Define realistic standards and conditions of performance,** specific and measurable performance indicators and skill/competency requirements for the job. This should take into account input from job-holders, resulting in a mutually acceptable and understood definition of what is expected of the individual or team, in the form of a performance agreement.

Step 3: **Draw up a detailed performance and development plan** with the collaboration and agreement of the individual or team concerned. This is essentially a problem-solving action plan, detailing areas of performance identified as requiring improvement, training needs, improvement proposals and development opportunities.

Step 4: **Monitor, evaluate, discuss and adjust performance on a continual basis.** Regular reviews of performance are used as opportunities to exchange feedback in order to adjust work plans or targets, reward successful performance, plan control action or identify on-going development opportunities.

Step 5: Review performance at the end of the agreed period (say, annually).

(b) **Benefits to employees**

Given the constructive, forward-looking and collaborative aspects of performance management, its advantages should be as follows.

(i) **Security**: knowing exactly what is expected and (having agreed targets) that it is realistically achievable.

(ii) **Opportunity** to be involved in problem-solving and adding value: a source of job satisfaction.

(iii) Opportunities for **learning and development**.

(iv) Managerial commitment to support performance with resources, training, improvements in systems and working methods and so on: making the job better.

(v) Constructive orientation: absence of negative/punitive and judgemental aspects of appraisal.

BPP PUBLISHING

Marking guide

Marks

Section A

1 (a) 'What is happening   5
        Reasons why   5
                                                            10

   (b) Tactics
        Conflicting parties   5
        Management response   7
                                                            12

   (c) Managing conflict
        Ecological   4
        Regulation   4
        Motivation issues   2
                                                            10

   (d) Value of conflict
        Constructive   4
        Destructive   4
                                                             8
                                                            40

Section B

2 Explain term   3-4
                                                             3

   Four characteristics (two per characteristic)   8-10
                                                             8

   Barrier to learning (one per barrier)   4
                                                             4
                                                            15

3 (a) Job description   1
        Person specification   1
        Difference   2
                                                             4

   (b) Contents   5
                                                             5

   (c) Uses and limitations   3
        Uses   3
                                                             6
                                                            15

4 (a) Delegation   5-6
                                                             5

   (b) (i)   Delegation downwards   5-6
                                                             5

        (ii) Delegation upwards   5-6
                                                             5
                                                            15

5 (a) Description grid   5-6
                                                             5

   (b) Four extremes (one for each identified)   4
                                                             4

   (c) Usefulness   6-7
                                                             6
                                                            15

6 (a) Definition   1-2
        Distinction from personnel   1-2
        Steps (max 2 per step)   6-8
                                                            10

   (b) Advantages (1 per advantage)   5
                                                             5
                                                            15

108

Managing People
BPP Mock Exam 2:
Pilot Paper

Question Paper:	
Time allowed	**3 hours**
This paper is divided into two sections	
Section A	This question is compulsory and MUST be attempted
Section B	FOUR questions ONLY to be answered

paper 1.3

DO NOT OPEN THIS PAPER UNTIL YOU ARE READY TO START
UNDER EXAMINATION CONDITIONS

Section A - This section is compulsory and MUST be attempted

1   Deborah Williams, the finance director of SMG Ltd, thinks that the staff in the accounts department are overworked and has asked the Human Resource Department for an additional accounts clerk, preferably two.

SMG has no formal procedures or processes to ensure that appropriate and qualified staff are appointed. In the past SMG Ltd has relied on agencies and informal contacts to recruit new employees.

SMG Ltd has recently appointed you as assistant Human Resource Manager. You have been asked to take charge of the situation, to see if Ms Williams has a case and then to manage the new appointments process if the vacancy is approved.

Required

(a)   Explain how you would establish whether Deborah Williams has a legitimate case for a new member of staff.   (8 marks)

(b)   Given that the vacancy is approved, discuss the procedure you would take to appoint a qualified accounts clerk.   (7 marks)

(c)   Describe the contents of a job description and person specification for the new accounts clerk.   (10 marks)

(d)   Explain how you would carry out the recruitment and selection of the new clerk.
                                                                            (10 marks)

(e)   What might be the benefits of ongoing training and development to the clerk and the business?   (5 marks)
                                                                            (40 marks)

Section B – Answer any FOUR questions. ALL questions carry equal marks.

2   A team differs from an informal work group.

Required

(a) Explain the way in which a team differs from an informal work group.   (5 marks)

(b) Describe any five factors required to ensure team success.   (10 marks)

(15 Marks)

3   The manager of the finance department has asked you to carry out a job analysis of the other employees in your department.

Required

(a) Briefly explain what is meant by the term 'job analysis'.   (3 marks)

(b) Briefly explain the four stages involved in carrying out a job analysis.   (4 marks)

(c) Identify and briefly explain the information you would expect to collect during the job analysis investigation.   (8 marks)

(15 marks)

4   Different learning styles and approaches suit different individuals.

Required

(a) Identify and explain Honey & Mumford's theory on learning styles.   (10 marks)

(b) Explain the experiential learning cycle.   (5 marks)

(15 Marks)

5   Financial rewards are not appropriate in all circumstances.

Required

(a) Briefly explain what is meant by **intrinsic** rewards.   (3 marks)

(b) Briefly explain what is meant by **extrinsic** rewards.   (3 marks)

(c) List any six types of extrinsic reward.   (9 marks)

(15 marks)

6   Much of the work of professional accountants involves communicating information for others to use.

Required

(a) Explain the importance of clear communication.   (5 marks)

(b) Explain two main communication methods.   (5 marks)

(c) Describe two barriers to communication.   (5 marks)

(15 marks)

ANSWERS

DO NOT TURN THIS PAGE UNTIL YOU
HAVE COMPLETED THE MOCK EXAM

WARNING! APPLYING THE BPP MARKING SCHEME

If you decide to mark your paper using the BPP marking scheme, you should bear in mind the following points.

1   The BPP solutions are not definitive: you will see that we have applied the marking scheme to our solutions to show how good answers should gain marks, but there may be more than one way to answer the question. You must try to judge fairly whether different points made in your answers are correct and relevant and therefore worth marks according to our marking scheme.

2   If you have a friend or colleague who is studying or has studied this paper, you might ask him or her to mark your paper for you, thus gaining a more objective assessment. Remember you and your friend are not trained or objective markers, so try to avoid complacency or pessimism if you appear to have done very well or very badly.

3   You should be aware that BPP's answers are longer than you would be expected to write. Sometimes, therefore, you would gain the same number of marks for making the basic point as we have shown as being available for a slightly more detailed or extensive solution.

It is most important that you analyse your solutions in detail and that you attempt to be as objective as possible.

PLAN OF ATTACK

Managing People is a 'wordy' subject, without the clear 'yes' and 'no' answers you can achieve in the other papers at this level. That doesn't mean that you can waffle your way to a pass in your sleep, but there are plenty of easy marks if you have done the reading.

The keys to passing this paper are:

- Using the knowledge you have – you can't rely on 'common sense'; the questions are often factual, and the scenario will expect you to apply theory and background knowledge.

- Time management – Section A should take 72 minutes, maximum and each of the section B questions should take 27 minutes. (So, if you start Section A at 2pm, you should have finished at 3.12pm.)

- Clear presentation of your answers

Read the rubric. You must do question A, and you have to do four out of five questions in Section B. So your **only** choices are:

- The **order** in which you do the questions

- Which **one** of the Section B questions you **don't** want to do

Looking through the paper:

Section A is a straightforward scenario about recruitment and induction in a context which, hopefully, will be familiar. It covers Part B of the syllabus, from human resource planning, recruitment selection and induction training. Each of these questions was covered with a reasonable number of marks, and so Section A is a good scenario to start with with.

In this paper, therefore, we recommend you do Section A first – bear in mind your need to manage your time.

Section B offers more. Question 3 on job analysis covers, in more, depth the recruitment issue covered in Section A, and you might feel that if you are on a roll from Section A, that this is a useful question.

Otherwise Section B appears quite bitty. Question 2 is a theoretical question on teams and groups; note that you must **describe** factors for team success not just list them. Similarly, book knowledge on learning theory is tested at a fairly simple level in Question 4.

Question 5 on rewards ought to be a gift – 9 marks for a simple list of extrinsic rewards –and it appears to be a simple list. If you have forgotten the difference between intrinsic and extrinsic rewards and get them switched round – and you might do in the heat of the exam – you will get it totally wrong. But otherwise, these 9 marks must be the easiest in this exam!

And time management?

The mark allocations should influence the time you have available. If you do things too quickly, particularly in the apparently simple questions, you may not be going into enough depth. Beware of exceeding the time limit – but beware, too, of overconfidence – if you finish the exam with an hour to spare, you probably haven't written enough.

1   ACCOUNTS CLERK

> **Tutor's hint.** This question covers the entire process of recruitment and selection from HR planning to HR development – a very substantial portion of the syllabus. Part (a) required you to think carefully about Deborah's situation. Managers have to think how matters can be done better. Before taking on a new member of staff, it would seem logical to see other ways by which this activity can be resourced. Parts (b), (c) and (d) refer more to the 'knowledge' in the syllabus.

(a)   **Deborah's case for a new staff member**

Staff are a major element of **cost** and headcount should be subject to careful control. In a large, mature organisation with established procedures and methods, the **human resource plan** or establishment document would lay down the staff requirements for the accounts department.

Permission to recruit would depend on either a member of staff having left (staff **turnover**), or the **expansion of the department's task**. The latter might result from organisational growth or, particularly in the case of an accounts department, from the increasing burden of government-imposed work, as with the maintenance of working time records, for instance. Where the task had expanded, the human resource plan would have to be amended.

However, SMG Limited 'has no formal procedures or processes' for recruitment and, therefore, reference to an agreed establishment is not possible. It will be for Deborah Williams to demonstrate just why she thinks that the accounts staff are overworked before recruitment is authorised.

Another way would be to look to see if the accounts department can be run more efficiently. An examination of its procedures would be extremely time consuming and probably beyond the capacity of a human resources specialist. However, it may be possible to carry out a job analysis in broad terms if the department is not too large. This would attempt to measure the volume and nature of the work flowing through the office by collecting information from four sources:

- Documentation, such as forms and instructions
- Interviews with managers and supervisors
- Interviews with job holders
- Observation

If it is found that this is not possible, the **fall-back position would be for Deborah Williams to justify the recruitment in concrete terms**. However, because Deborah Williams is a **director** of the company, a recently appointed assistant manager in HR would find it difficult to demand such a justification. A suitable procedure would probably have to be established by agreement among the directors: perhaps Deborah has the authority anyway.

(b)   **Procedures to appoint a qualified accounts clerk**

Step 1.   Obtain agreement that there is a vacancy – already presupposed from the question.

Step 2.   Clearly detail the total mix of tasks to be carried out in the department, including work that is not being done owing to lack of resources.

Step 3.   Assess whether current employees have the competences currently to carry out all the tasks, or whether these can be developed.

Step 4. Assess whether the current allocation of work amongst employees genuinely reflects their competences. Could there be greater job specialisation?

Step 5. Assess the future needs of the department in terms of the quality and nature of competences required.

Step 6. Identify the mix of training and resourcing needs necessary to carry out the department's task.

Step 7. Develop or revise job descriptions based on the roles currently performed in the department. Existing members of staff will welcome clear descriptions of what is expected of them if roles are to change.

Step 8. Develop person specification as the basis of the recruitment and selection process, based on the job descriptions and required competences which are going to be met by recruitment.

Step 9. Develop plan for recruitment and selection of new staff, if this is the preferred way of matching the resource and competences of the department with the work expected of it.

Step 10. Implement the plan (see part (d) of this answer).

The process involves **two types of company policy.**

(i) The procedures manual, which deals with the steps gone through, any legal requirements (guaranteeing conformance with equal opportunities legislation)

(ii) The human resources plan, which details the overall requirements for employees, investment in training and so on.

(c) **Job description and person specification**

A **job description** is a statement of the tasks, responsibilities and working relationships making up a job. At lower levels it will concentrate on the specification of duties, but at managerial levels it is likely to be written in broader terms dealing with scope and responsibilities. It forms an important part of the documentation needed by a complex organisation, since, in combination with other job descriptions, it defines how work is done.

A **person specification** details the personal qualities, abilities, qualifications and experience required of the holder of a job. A job description is useful in several human resource management contexts, including recruitment, appraisal and career development. A person specification, on the other hand, is rarely useful for anything other than recruitment.

Since it is rare to find a perfect fit between any job and its holder, the task of recruitment is eased if the job description is divided into core and peripheral elements. This allows the features of the person specification to be divided into those that are essential and those that are merely desirable. This split makes it easier to select the best person for the job when no ideal candidate applies.

(d) **Recruitment and selection of the clerk**

The recruitment and selection process is based on the needs of the department, and the state of the labour market. There are a number of different steps. Once it has been decided that recruiting a new member of staff (rather than redeploying current members) is the right course then the following steps should be taken.

Step 1. Obtain job description, which details job content, responsibilities, and the job's relation to other positions in the department, authorisation limits. It might be phrased in more general terms as an accountability profile.

117

Step 2. If a person specification has not yet been drawn up, identify the type of candidate suitable for the job, noting essential attributes (eg for an accounts clerk post, the firm may require a candidate with the ACCA's Certified Accounting Technician qualification), desirable attributes (eg experience in a similar **company**) and contra-indications (ie matters that would rule out the candidate, for example no work experience at all).

Step 3. Identify appropriate media for recruitment. To reach the right people, the firm has to find the right medium.

The firm could use a **recruitment agency** to suggest suitable candidates already on their books, to do some preliminary screening and to suggest a shortlist.

The firm may choose to **advertise**. The job advertisement will cover details of the role and the company and should be targeted at the target candidates, with an attractive, but realistic, description of the company and role; salary details may also be included. Most importantly, contact details and the desired manner of application (eg letter and cv, or application form) must be made clear.

Step 4. Place the advertisement in suitable **publications** (such as newspapers, professional journals). The firm might also use **government employment offices** (job centres, in the UK). Moreover, firms are increasingly advertising on the **Internet**, either on their own websites or via recruitment services (often owned or run by newspaper groups) such as <u>workthing.com</u>.

Step 5. Review application forms/cvs received. As a matter of courtesy all applicants should receive a reply; some may be rejected out of hand; others may be told that their application has been received and is being reviewed. Application forms are a standard way of gathering data, for comparison, and also to require candidates to answer specific questions, to collect data about qualifications and experience and to allow the candidate to write about themselves and why the want the position.

Step 6. Shortlist desirable candidates and contact them to arrange interviews. Write to unsuccessful candidates

Step 7. **Interviews**

Most firms use the interview as the heart of their recruitment procedures even though it is not reliable as a predictor of job performance. It does enable a firm to assess some of the candidate's interpersonal skills. A mixture of open and closed questions should be used. The interview is also an opportunity for the candidate to talk about the role

Step 8. **Tests**

A variety of tests can be employed, often relating to the task to be done. This may be of limited relevance to an accounts position where work experience can be validated. However, it should be possible to assess basic numeracy. A person with a technician or professional qualification may have a training record which can be used as evidence of competence. More complicated tests (psychometric etc) are not appropriate for this position.

Step 9. **Make offer, subject to references**

References are of limited value, but they can be used to check the candidate's basic honesty (eg in seeing that the candidate's past employment history is truthful, that the candidate worked in a the positions and over the timescales mentioned).

The offer of employment may contain contractual details.

Step 10. **Induction**

When the new employee starts, he/she needs to become familiar with the firm.

(e) Training and development are usually regarded as two different things.

Training is the process by which workpeople are taught job-related skills.

Development is a more general process by which people are prepared for wider future responsibilities.

(i) While it will be possible to establish very specific training objectives and to measure progress towards them in some detail, the objectives of development are likely to be more conceptual and progress may take a variety of forms.

(ii) Both training and development are likely to offer benefits to the individual and to the organisation.

(iii) Increased job competence makes the organisation more efficient. It also reduces stress on the individual and is a source of pride and competence and hence of motivation. The achievement of a specific qualification or level of competence may entitle the individual to a pay rise.

(iv) Organisational flexibility is enhanced when staff are well trained, since they can deputise for absent colleagues and adapt rapidly to new procedures and other changing circumstances.

(v) A programme of personal development contributes to succession and promotion planning.

(vi) It helps with the identification of people with the potential for promotion.

(vii) It provides promotees with at least some of the knowledge and skills they will need, so that they can tackle their new responsibilities with confidence.

(viii) The efficiency of the organisation is thus enhanced, and the individuals concerned are advanced in their careers. Even if they are not promoted, they are likely to be more employable. This improves their job security within the organisation and their prospects elsewhere if they wish to move.

2   TEAM SUCCESS

> **Tutor's hint.** In Part (b) you could conceivably have gone into more detail about team roles and the mix of skills (Belbin). You could also have considered matters such as group think or conformity.

(a) While different from one another, informal work groups and teams are both **groups** and have shared attributes.

- Purpose and leadership
- A sense of identity
- Loyalty to the group

The differences between teams and informal work groups lie within these shared attributes and exist primarily because of the sharp distinction in **reason for existence**.

- **Teams** are established by an organisation to perform organisational tasks, often with an official leader.

- **Informal groups** come into existence in response to the social and personal needs of the members. This difference is reflected in the nature of the leadership exercised within the two types of group.

In an informal group, leadership is likely to be exercised in a more **fluid** way, possibly with several members sharing the leadership role. Satisfaction of group and individual needs will depend on individual initiatives by the more perceptive and influential members of the group. Loyalty and identification with the group may be very strong, but this is likely to result from commonality of personal interest rather than effective leadership.

(b) **A variety of factors will contribute to team success**

(i) **Leadership** is probably the most important single factor and the one most often lacking. Good leadership will promote co-operation between team members, motivate the individuals towards the task and ensure that work is properly organised.

A team is likely to have a **leader** appointed by the organisation and it is one of the tasks of leadership to promote the coherence of the group. This will include motivating, organising and controlling the efforts of individuals in pursuit of the team's work objectives; these are what *Adair* calls **task needs**.

Adair suggests that the leader should also pursue **individual needs** and **group needs**. The process of motivation is also an individual need, as are the requirements for recognition and counselling. Group needs include peacekeeping and standard setting. Successful leadership is likely to produce a sense of identity and loyalty to the team almost as by-products of the satisfaction of other group and individual needs.

(ii) The **task** or **role** of the team must be defined. This can be seen in terms of the objectives set for the leader, since the leader must take responsibility for the team's work.

(iii) The members of the team must possess the **right mix of skills** required for them to perform their roles. To some extent, these can be learned on the job, under the supervision of the leader.

(iv) A proper level of **resources** must be provided, though motivation can overcome many resource deficiencies.

(v) The efforts of the team must be **co-ordinated** with those of the rest of the organisation. To some extent this is a task for the leader, but there must be mechanisms in place to allow sideways communication between team members and other parts of the organisation and to permit proper response to changed circumstances.

3   JOB ANALYSIS

> **Tutor's hint.** Job analysis is about the job, not the performance of the person doing the job. However the 'location' of the job is also important – is it to be done as part of a team or in isolation?

(a) **Job analysis** is the process of examining a job to determine its essential characteristics, including its component tasks and the circumstances and constraints under which it is performed. It provides the basis for the preparation of a **job description** and may also contribute to a scheme of **job evaluation**.

(b) There are four main sources of information about a job. It would be sensible to approach them in the order given below.

   (i) There may be **documentation** such as written procedures, organisation charts, quality manuals and even earlier job descriptions. These can be consulted at leisure.

   (ii) An early approach to the relevant **supervisor** is advisable. This person is likely to have clear ideas about what the job includes and may be able to resolve subsequent queries.

   (iii) The **job-holder** should be consulted. What the person concerned thinks the job consists of is likely to differ noticeably both from what the supervisor thinks is done and from what the documentation says should be done.

   (iv) A possible final stage is **observation** of what the job-holder **actually does**. Once again, this may differ from what the job-holder has described.

   (v) A full picture of the job will emerge from these four sources. An important task for the analyst is to establish what adjustments need to be made to the documentation and whether extra activities that have developed should be done elsewhere.

(c) **Job analysis should produce information that relates to both the job.**

   Job-related information should start with the overall **purpose and scope** of the job. This sets the job in its organisational context and should be stated briefly. For example, the scope of an accounts clerk's job might be to maintain ledgers on a computerised system. Direct accountability may be included at this stage by stating the supervisor to whom the job-holder reports

   It will then be appropriate to list the specific **duties and responsibilities** of the job, setting them out in logical groups. For instance, it would be sensible to list all the duties relating to the purchase ledger separately from those relating to the sales ledger. **Performance** criteria should be included.

   Duties and **responsibilities** may be discussed together or separately, depending on the nature of the job. However, it is important to include information on the levels of responsibility held for staff, money, equipment and other resources.

   The **environment** and **conditions** of the job should be investigated. This includes such factors such as pay and benefits, shift work and holidays. Particular attention should be paid to the physical environment and to potential hazards.

   The **social factors** relating to the job should be stated. This will include whether it is done in isolation or as part of a team; the level in the organisation at which the job-holder interacts; and whether there is external contact, as with customers, for instance.

4   **LEARNING STYLE**

> **Tutor's hint.** Again fairly straightforward.

(a) **Honey and Mumford**

   The way in which people learn best will differ according to the type of person. That is, there are learning styles which suit different individuals. Peter Honey and Alan Mumford have drawn up a popular classification of four learning styles.

(i) **Theorists** seek to understand basic principles and to take an intellectual, 'hands-off' approach based on logical argument. They prefer training to be:

- Programmed and structured
- Designed to allow time for analysis
- Provided by teachers who share his/her preference for concepts and analysis

(ii) **Reflectors**

- Observe phenomena, think about them and then choose how to act
- Need to work at their own pace
- Find learning difficult if forced into a hurried programme
- Produce carefully thought-out conclusions after research and reflection
- Tend to be fairly slow, non-participative (unless to ask questions) and cautious

(iii) **Activists**

- Deal with practical, active problems and do not have patience with theory
- Require training based on hands-on experience
- Are excited by participation and pressure, such as new projects
- Flexible and optimistic, but tend to rush at something without due preparation

(iv) **Pragmatists**

- Only like to study if they can see its direct link to practical problems
- Good at learning new techniques in on-the-job training
- Aim is to implement action plans and/or do the task better
- May discard good ideas which only require some development

Training programmes should ideally be designed to accommodate the preferences of all four styles. This can often be overlooked especially as the majority of training staff are activists.

(b) **Kolb** suggests that effective learning takes place in a cycle of four phases.

(i) The first stage is to be involved in a new experience.

(ii) The second stage is to review and reflect upon the experience.

(iii) The third stage is to use concepts and theories to integrate the experience and the reflection.

(iv) The final stage is one of application: to make use of the integrated for planning and decision making in new situations involving new experiences. Kolb felt that some people have a preference for a particular phase and so do not complete the cycle. They thus do not learn as effectively as they might. Honey and Mumford identified four learning styles that correspond to the four phases of Kolb's cycle and can be used to design effective learning events.

5   REWARDS

> **Tutor's hint**. An incredibly easy question especially part (c): 9 marks for a simple list you could jot down in half the time. But remember you were asked to list extrinsic rewards. If you listed 'recognition' or 'fulfilment' in the list, this would have been incorrect.

(a) **Intrinsic rewards** are those which arise from the performance of the work itself. They are therefore psychological rather than material and relate to the concept of job satisfaction. Intrinsic rewards include the satisfaction that comes from completing a piece of work, the status that certain jobs convey, the feeling of achievement that comes from doing a difficult job well. Intrinsic rewards tend to be associated with **autonomy** in the planning and execution of work.

(b) **Extrinsic rewards** are separate from the job itself and dependent on the decisions of others. Pay, benefits and working conditions are all examples of extrinsic rewards.

(c) **Rewards**

- Pay
- Bonuses
- A car
- Medical insurance
- Pension scheme
- Subsidised canteen facilities
- Working clothing such as uniform, but not safety equipment
- Share option schemes
- Subsidised loans and mortgages
- Subsidised transport to and from work
- Assistance with child care
- Holiday entitlement

6   COMMUNICATION

Tutor's hint. Note in part (b) that we distinguish between **methods** and **media**. Email, for example, as a medium for text-based, or written, communication.

(a) Communication is the process of **transferring information** from one person to another. In an organisational context, communication may be internal, as when colleagues discuss a problem, or it may be that the participants are representatives of their organisations, as when a credit control manager writes to a named manager in an overdue debtor organisation.

Organisations exist to achieve goals which individuals could not achieve independently. Communication is therefore **fundamental** to their operations. The classic managerial functions of planning, organising, directing and controlling depend on the manager's ability to communicate requirements and information and to obtain reports. Other management responsibilities such as motivating, training and counselling depend equally upon clear communication.

It is in the general area of human behaviour and relations that **manner, tone and body language** become important supplements to the written or spoken word. This applies equally to managers and to members of work groups who must communicate with one another.

If communication is not clear, there will be bias, omission and distortion. Confusion, conflict and stress arise as a result.

(b) The two main **methods** of communication are **speech** and **writing**. Both may be used between individuals, as in the interview or personal letter, or by an individual to more than one person, as in the lecture or circulated memo.

The two basic methods vary in their effect and usefulness in different situations. Speech is immediate and tone, manner and body language can be used to enhance its impact. Feedback can be instant and a disciplined discussion can cover a lot of ground rapidly. The written word is easier to use with precision, though this takes time,

BPP PUBLISHING

practise and ability. It is inherently capable of repeated reference using the simplest technology; speech requires electronic equipment such as a video system if its full impact is to be recorded.

A wide range of **media** may be used for both spoken and written communications. Some are listed below.

Speech may be used face-to-face, on the telephone, on video (including video conferencing) on public address and loudspeaker systems and on radio broadcast.

Writing is used in paper communications of all kinds, including letters, memos, procedure manuals, forms and books. It is also used in e-mail, fax and telex systems and in pager systems.

(c)   Good communication is essential to getting any job done: co-operation is impossible without it.

(i)   Difficulties occur because of **general faults** in the communication process

- Distortion or omission of information by the sender

- Misunderstanding due to lack of clarity or technical jargon

- Non-verbal signs (gesture, posture, facial expression) contradicting the verbal message, so that its meaning is in doubt

- 'Overload' - a person being given too much information to digest in the time available

- Differences in social, racial or educational background, compounded by age and personality differences, creating barriers to understanding and co-operation

- People hearing only what they want to hear in a message

(ii)   There may also be **particular difficulties** in a work situation

- A general tendency to distrust a message in its re-telling from one person to another, (eg a subordinate mistrusting his superior and looking for 'hidden meanings' in a message).

- The relative status in the hierarchy of the sender and receiver of information (a senior manager's words are listened to more closely and a colleague's perhaps discounted).

- People from different job or specialist backgrounds (accountants, personnel managers, DP experts) having difficulty in talking on a non-specialist's wavelength.

- People or departments having different priorities or perspectives so that one person places more or less emphasis on a situation than another.

- Conflict in the organisation. Where there is conflict between individuals or departments, communications will be withdrawn and information withheld.

Marking guide

			Marks
Section A			
1	(a)	Identification of general background	4
		Identification and description of job analysis	4
			8
	(b)	Description of formal process (one mark per step)	10
			10
	(c)	Contents of job description for this vacancy	4
		Contents of person specification for this vacancy	3
			7
	(d)	Explanation of procedure involved in the recruitment and selection of the new clerk (max. two marks for each stage)	10
			10
	(e)	Recognition and description of benefits (One mark each)	$\underline{5}$
			5
			$\underline{\underline{40}}$

Section B			
2	(a)	Explanation of differences (One mark each)	5-6
			5
	(b)	Description of factors (One mark each)	$\underline{10\text{-}12}$
			10
			$\underline{\underline{15}}$

3	(a)	Explanation of the term 'job analysis'	3-4
			3
	(b)	Description and discussion of the four steps (One mark per step)	4-5
			4
	(c)	Description and discussion of the information expected (One mark per topic)	$\underline{8\text{-}10}$
			8
			$\underline{\underline{15}}$

4	(a)	Identification of each of the four learning styles. (Two marks per style, two marks floating for description)	10-12
			10
	(b)	Description of the experimental learning cycle	$\underline{5\text{-}6}$
			5
			$\underline{\underline{15}}$

5	(a)	Explanation of intrinsic awards	3-4
			3
	(b)	Explanation of extrinsic awards	3-4
			3
	(c)	Description of six examples of extrinsic rewards (One and a half marks per reward)	$\underline{9\text{-}10}$
			9
			$\underline{\underline{15}}$

6	(a)	Brief explanation of the importance of clear communication (one mark each)	5-7
			5
	(b)	Actual forms of communication (one mark each)	5-7
			5
	(c)	Identification and explanation (one mark per barrier identified)	$\underline{5\text{-}7}$
			5
			$\underline{\underline{15}}$

See overleaf for information on other
BPP products and how to order

ACCA Order - New Syllabus

To BPP Publishing Ltd, Aldine Place, London W12 8AA
Tel: 020 8740 2211. Fax: 020 8740 1184
email: publishing@bpp.com
online: www.bpp.com

Mr/Mrs/Ms (Full name)

Daytime delivery address

Postcode

Date of exam (month/year)

Daytime Tel

	2/01 Texts	8/01 Kits	9/01 Passcards	MCQ cards	Tapes	Videos
PART 1						
1.1 Preparing Financial Statements	£19.95	£10.95	£5.95	£5.95	£12.95	£25.00
1.2 Financial Information for Management	£19.95	£10.95	£5.95	£5.95	£12.95	£25.00
1.3 Managing People	£19.95	£10.95	£5.95		£12.95	£25.00
PART 2						
2.1 Information Systems	£19.95	£10.95	£5.95		£12.95	£25.00
2.2 Corporate and Business Law (6/01)	£19.95	£10.95	£5.95		£12.95	£25.00
2.3 Business Taxation FA 2000 (for 12/01 exam)	£19.95	£10.95 (4/01)	£5.95 (4/01)		£12.95	£25.00
2.4 Financial Management and Control	£19.95	£10.95	£5.95		£12.95	£25.00
2.5 Financial Reporting (6/01)	£19.95	£10.95	£5.95		£12.95	£25.00
2.6 Audit and Internal Review (6/01)	£19.95	£10.95	£5.95		£12.95	£25.00
PART 3						
3.1 Audit and Assurance Services (6/01)	£20.95	£10.95	£5.95		£12.95	£25.00
3.2 Advanced Taxation FA 2000 (for 12/01 exam)	£20.95	£10.95 (4/01)	£5.95 (4/01)		£12.95	£25.00
3.3 Performance Management	£20.95	£10.95	£5.95		£12.95	£25.00
3.4 Business Information Management	£20.95	£10.95	£5.95		£12.95	£25.00
3.5 Strategic Business Planning and Development	£20.95	£10.95	£5.95		£12.95	£25.00
3.6 Advanced Corporate Reporting (6/01)	£20.95	£10.95	£5.95		£12.95	£25.00
3.7 Strategic Financial Management	£20.95	£10.95	£5.95		£12.95	£25.00
INTERNATIONAL STREAM						
1.1 Preparing Financial Statements	£19.95	£10.95	£5.95	£5.95	£12.95	£25.00
2.5 Financial Reporting (6/01)	£19.95	£10.95	£5.95		£12.95	£25.00
2.6 Audit and Internal Review (6/01)	£19.95	£10.95	£5.95		£12.95	£25.00
3.1 Audit and Assurance services (6/01)	£20.95	£10.95	£5.95		£12.95	£25.00
3.6 Advanced Corporate Reporting (6/01)	£20.95	£10.95	£5.95		£12.95	£25.00
SUCCESS IN YOUR RESEARCH AND ANALYSIS PROJECT						
Tutorial Text (9/00) (new edition 9/01)	£19.95					

SUBTOTAL £

POSTAGE & PACKING

Study Texts

	First	Each extra	
UK	£3.00	£2.00	£
Europe*	£5.00	£4.00	£
Rest of world	£20.00	£10.00	£

Kits/Passcards/Success Tapes/MCQ cards

	First	Each extra	
UK	£2.00	£1.00	£
Europe*	£2.50	£1.00	£
Rest of world	£15.00	£8.00	£

Breakthrough Videos

	First	Each extra	
UK	£2.00	£2.00	£
Europe*	£2.00	£2.00	£
Rest of world	£20.00	£10.00	£

Grand Total (Cheques to *BPP Publishing*) I enclose
a cheque for (incl. Postage) £

Or charge to Access/Visa/Switch

Card Number

Expiry date   Start Date

Issue Number (Switch Only)

Signature

We aim to deliver to all UK addresses inside 5 working days; a signature will be required. Orders to all EU addresses should be delivered within 6 working days. All other orders to overseas addresses should be delivered within 8 working days. * Europe includes the Republic of Ireland and the Channel Islands.

REVIEW FORM & FREE PRIZE DRAW

All original review forms from the entire BPP range, completed with genuine comments, will be entered into one of two draws 31 January 2002 and 31 July 2002. The names on the first four forms picked out on each occasion will be sent a cheque for £50.

Name: _____   Address: _____

_____

_____

How have you used this Kit?
(Tick one box only)

☐ Self study (book only)

☐ On a course: college (please state)_____

_____

☐ With 'correspondence' package

☐ Other _____

Why did you decide to purchase this Kit? *(Tick one box only)*

☐ Have used the complementary Study Text

☐ Have used other BPP products in the past

☐ Recommendation by friend/colleague

☐ Recommendation by a lecturer at college

☐ Saw advertising in journals

☐ Saw website

☐ Other _____

During the past six months do you recall seeing/receiving any of the following?
(Tick as many boxes as are relevant)

☐ Our advertisement in *Student Accountant*

☐ Our advertisement in *Pass*

☐ Our brochure with a letter through the post

☐ Our website

Which (if any) aspects of our advertising do you find useful?
(Tick as many boxes as are relevant)

☐ Prices and publication dates of new editions

☐ Information on product content

☐ Facility to order books off-the-page

☐ None of the above

When did you sit the exam? _____

Which of the following BPP products have you used for this paper?

☐ Study Text ☐ MCQ Cards ☑ Kit ☐ Passcards ☐ Success Tape ☐ Breakthrough Video

Your ratings, comments and suggestions would be appreciated on the following areas of this Kit.

	Very useful	Useful	Not useful
'Question search tools'	☐	☐	☐
'The exam'	☐	☐	☐
'Background'	☐	☐	☐
Preparation questions	☐	☐	☐
Exam standard questions	☐	☐	☐
'Tutor's hints' section in answers	☐	☐	☐
Content and structure of answers	☐	☐	☐
Mock exams	☐	☐	☐
'Plan of attack'	☐	☐	☐
Mock exam answers	☐	☐	☐

	Excellent	Good	Adequate	Poor
Overall opinion of this Kit	☐	☐	☐	☐

Do you intend to continue using BPP products?   ☐ Yes   ☐ No

Please note any further comments and suggestions/errors on the reverse of this page. The BPP author of this edition can be e-mailed at: edmundhewson@bpp.com

Please return this form to: Katy Hibbert, ACCA range manager, BPP Publishing Ltd, FREEPOST, London, W12 8BR

REVIEW FORM & FREE PRIZE DRAW (continued)

Please note any further comments and suggestions/errors below.

FREE PRIZE DRAW RULES

1   Closing date for 31 January 2002 draw is 31 December 2001. Closing date for 31 July 2002 draw is 30 June 2002.

2   Restricted to entries with UK and Eire addresses only. BPP employees, their families and business associates are excluded.

3   No purchase necessary. Entry forms are available upon request from BPP Publishing. No more than one entry per title, per person. Draw restricted to persons aged 16 and over.

4   Winners will be notified by post and receive their cheques not later than 6 weeks after the relevant draw date.

5   The decision of the promoter in all matters is final and binding. No correspondence will be entered into.